The Power of

Mental Wealth

Featuring

Deirdre Goveia

The Power of Mental Wealth

Featuring Deirdre Goveia

Success Begins From Within

Deirdre Goveia

Johnny Wimbrey

Heather Monahan

Les Brown

WIMBREY TRAINING SYSTEMS
SOUTHLAKE, TEXAS

Published by Wimbrey Training Systems
550 Reserve Street, Suite 190
Southlake, Texas 76092

Printed in the United States of America

ISBN: 978-1-951502-42-3

Table of Contents

Foreword

The world has become a more unpredictable and threatening place over the last year. Our ability to survive and thrive has been tested by tremendous outside forces that aren't in our control. Among the few things we *can* control are our perceptions and our thoughts.

The Power of Mental Wealth is a book I'm very proud to publish, especially at this moment in human history. This is a time for us to invest in our minds and not squander our mental resources.

Mental *wealth* is a cutting edge-concept, one you may not have heard much about just yet. The concept of mental wealth is just beginning to gain traction as people start to realize its possibilities and immense value.

So how is it different from mental health? Or mental strength? Is it something you can bring to the bank?

More than twenty immensely talented people share their definitions of this term and their mental gifts with you in *The Power of Mental Wealth*. Their chapters include stories of perseverance, overcoming adversities, building self-confidence, increasing their joy, and training themselves to see the brilliance and success of their futures.

In every single case, they worked hard to perfect themselves and improve their minds. They worked on this intensely, investing a good chunk of their time, for years. They all succeeded, and so can you.

Not one of these authors suggests their gifts were just handed to them. They built their mental wealth the old-fashioned way, and they're sharing their results with you. They share the tools they use, such as listening, using their subconscious or all their senses, and building self-worth. They've learned to believe in themselves, create their own realities, and live life by design.

They have mastered the power of their wills.

I am awed by their potential, and even more, awed by their generosity in sharing what they've learned with you.

You can build your mental wealth through what you learn in this book. As world-famous Les Brown writes in his chapter, *grow continuously*.

Invest in your mind. It's the best investment you can make.

—Johnny Wimbrey

Chapter 1

The Power of Your Will

Johnny Wimbrey

They say a mind is a terrible thing to waste. I'll take this further: I say it's terrible, even unforgivable if you don't commit yourself to strengthening your mental powers and turning them into your strongest assets.

And, honestly, I'm amazed every day by the potential we all have. We are the only beings with the power of self-will. This means that we all possess the mental capacity to obey or to disobey, to lie or to be honest, to love or to hate, and the mental strength to will ourselves past adverse situations to reach our goals. (Setting those goals is a whole other book; I'll tell you about Building a Millionaire Mindset later in this chapter.

None of us are immune to adversity, none are immune to temptation, and none are immune to life's trials and tribulations. Whether we'd like to admit it or not, we all fall short in life at one point or another. Every human being will experience the good, the bad, and the ugly. That's the reality of life. Some situations may seem very small and trivial to most people, but these trivial situations can and do escalate to very regrettable and drastic situations.

We all have faults.

They say confession is good for the soul, so let me come clean to you:

I have no tolerance for people who are late or situations that waste time. I can't stand to be late, and I hate being unproductive. I cherish time because it's irreplaceable; you can never get it back once it's gone. People who are not time-conscious frustrate me. Actually, they drive me crazy.

> *We can develop the mental wealth to be able to afford our dreams, and the mental strength to keep us on track.*

I wasn't born watching a clock; I programmed myself to be time-conscious a long time ago when I was very young. You may be thinking, What's wrong with this? Valuing time is a strength, an excellent tool for someone with ambition, especially for a leader. I agree in principle—but what's also a strength is being able to control your reactions, your will.

Anything you don't master will master you. My reaction to wasted or lost time is an emotion I can almost always control now, but for a few years, I struggled. When I lost my cool, it wasn't acceptable to me or to anyone who was unfortunate enough to be involved. It's a self-inflicted weakness, and it always embarrassed me. This was a real problem for me and others during my twenties.

The problem originally started when I changed my attitude about time. I didn't have the foresight to imagine having to cope with situations that were out of my control. I didn't realize even capable people (like me, I like to think) can make drastically bad decisions when we're not prepared for an unpredictable change that's completely out of our control.

Then one day I took control of my mind and things changed. It was a beautiful, sunny Texas day, I was driving my BMW roadster down an uncrowded road, cruising along, not too fast, with the convertible top down. Good music was playing on the audio system; I was at peace and in the very best of moods.

When I looked up and realized I'd missed my exit, everything changed in a heartbeat. My smile became a snarl and I could feel my blood pressure soar. My peaceful mood exploded into frustration and anger in a matter of seconds. Missing the exit may sound trivial, but you must understand, by the time I got back on course, I lost time—at least a whole five or ten minutes. I found this totally unacceptable.

As you read this, you're probably laughing at me, but I promise you, I'm not exaggerating my instinctive reaction. What's even more ridiculous is that I'd already been conducting seminars and self-help courses around the country. I'd studied a variety of philosophies, and had participated—as a leader!—in several seminars on self-control. And here I was frustrated and out of control because I had missed my exit.

I got off the highway and detoured through back streets to get back on course. As I drove, I began to think about something I had recently heard. It was still fresh in my mind, and for some reason, it really resonated with me:

If you want to get over a negative situation, begin to find positive things within your negative situation.

I figured, "What the heck? I have nothing else to do; let's see if it works." Though I was awash in my negativity and frustration, I began to look for positive things. At first, I didn't see any, so I began to look for simple things. You could call them simple pleasures.

I remember this next moment so clearly, it could have been yesterday. As I drove up to a red light and stopped, I looked at a car turning toward me from the side street. The driver was smiling, a wide, ecstatic grin. I said to myself, "If I hadn't missed my exit, I would never have seen that great grin."

Instantly, like magic, my frustration vanished. I thought, "Man, this is cool." And when the light turned green, I realized the light wasn't your normal green. The light glowed with a brilliant, rich, fluorescent green. And I thought to myself, "That's the most phenomenal green light I have ever seen. If I hadn't missed my exit, I would never have been able to experience this beautiful green light."

Now I must admit all of this was totally out of character for me, but it worked. I began to feel excited, almost as if I were in a competition to find positive things. It was fun!

I'd made a conscious decision to mentally master my out-of-control, overreacting battle against wasted time. Since that moment with the grin and the green light, I've only blown my top over lost time a couple of times. That doesn't mean I've mellowed to the point where it doesn't bother me. Of course, it does! I just control my thoughts, my willpower, and practice my mental strength.

Every individual has the ability to consciously decide whether to master a situation or to be mastered by it. Every individual also has the ability to decide how long he or she chooses to either master or be mastered by a situation.

There is a time and a season for everything. It is very important that you also understand every season will and must come to an end. As I conduct self-development training and seminars around the world, it amazes me to find only 10 percent of most individuals' mental battles are caused by the

5

situation. 90 percent of their struggles are caused by their inability to move on and simply let go of the problem, the habit, or whatever needs to be in the past. I find it difficult to watch a person wrestle with something that would immediately disappear if they could just simply let it go. It drives me crazy to see an individual be overwhelmed and mastered by a ridiculously simple situation, and I find it hard to be in their presence.

I'm working on my shortcoming of patience in this case, too, and I know soon I'll be more accepting of their idiotic reactions. But until I succeed in overcoming my aggravation at their bone-headed obtuseness, there are quite a few wonderful people whom I avoid because they, unfortunately, choose to be mastered by preposterous situations. To me, this is a form of mental bankruptcy.

For instance, how can two otherwise loving individuals be willing to have their marriage come to an end because they can't agree on whether the toilet paper roll should be hung with the paper over or under the roll? How could a person be a loving wife and mother one moment and the next moment be booked for homicide because road rage made her lose her mind?

Okay, I admit I made these up. Toilet paper has probably never been the cause of any divorce (except during the pandemic), and road rage can never be an acceptable alibi for murder.

But let's agree on this concept: Good people make bad decisions when they forfeit the right to master an obstacle or adversity and instead allow it to master them. It's said that you can always measure the character of a person by the size of the obstacle it takes to overcome him.

Good people become murderers every day—and good people are murdered every day—because of individuals who simply are not in control of their emotions. Think about it: How many people do you think are dead or in prison either because of their middle finger or someone else's middle finger? I don't truly know the answer, but isn't it ridiculous to think that a middle finger could cause an individual's rage to escalate to the point of deadly force? How hard would it be for most people to prepare or train themselves never to allow someone else's physical gestures to control them?

These days, different political preferences have caused apparently irreparable rifts in families and between friends. Are people going to avoid their best friend or brother forever because a yard sign, a comment, or a social media post made them blow up? Just because the country is not as bipartisan as it should be is no reason they can't have the generosity, love, and the will to accept different viewpoints. They can summon a smile as they work on negative reactions and keep their blood pressure under control.

What and who push your buttons and have the ability to cause you to lose control and step out of your character? When you hear the words "lose control," it's probably a natural instinct to think of individuals who are literally out of their minds or crazy. We hear these phrases all the time: "He really went off the deep end this time," "She just lost it," or "He just flipped." These are extreme examples, but we lose control every day without having the excuse of real mental illness.

Individuals who are not conscious of the fact that they are capable of losing control will adopt the habit of losing control. And one who adopts the habit of losing control creates the lifestyle of one who's out of control.

On the positive side, control can be regained. If you ever said, "I can't believe I just said that," or "I apologize for snapping like that," you were actively regaining control. You were making a deposit into your mental wealth account, and the next time around, it'll be even easier to recover your equilibrium.

Are you conscious of the moments where you're less in control, and willing to clearly accept and admit that you're being mastered?

I was once told that you should manage your weaknesses and master your strengths. I'm not saying we can ever be successful at mastering all of our emotions and every situation, but I am saying every successful step forward is a step toward being the master rather than being mastered. I believe if you practice mastering the basics—or what some would call the minor things in life—you are actively positioning yourself to avoid potential disasters. You are developing your will.

Is it possible to be in control in a very intense and heated situation? Absolutely! Let me give you an example.

Have you ever seen an NFL highlight special? It's like an R-rated version of a Super Bowl highlight special; there's no editing, and you can clearly hear everything the football players are saying on and off the field. It's mind-boggling to see a 300-pound man tackle another 300-pound man on the field, watch them both crash down onto the ground with one on top of the other, faces distorted with rage, screaming insults and yelling into each other's faces, close enough to feel the spit. Then the referee blows his whistle, and bam, it's all over. They help each other up, perhaps even with a friendly pat, and walk back to their huddles as though the tackle never happened.

How can a warrior type of guy, someone who is so revved up with total focus and intense energy, filled with competitive emotions, regain complete emotional, physical, and mental control in a nanosecond, just with a signal?

Do you know what's really crazy? That same football player with the willpower and discipline to walk away from someone who's spitting in his face and screaming insults while slamming him to the ground is the same guy who gets arrested the next week for a bar fight with a drunken football fan who calls him a loser.

Could this be the same person? And by the way, aren't legal penalties for breaking a drunken

9

loudmouth's head more severe than a ten-yard penalty from the NFL?

For years, these players have been mentally conditioned by their coaches; they completely understand that the consequences and penalties coming from uncontrollable behavior on the field are simply not worth the risk. The mental conditioning is at least as important as the physical training. Their results speak for themselves. Many of them just don't carry this discipline out into the rest of their lives. They don't see it as an asset they can use wherever they are—a form of mental wealth.

The questions to ask yourself are these:

Who's coaching you to understand the adversities you will face in the real world?

Who's teaching you how to evaluate the risks?

Who's teaching you how to control your mind and develop your will?

Who are your mentors?

Let me repeat: We are the only creatures with the gift of self-will. This means that we do possess the capacity and the power to control our minds. We can develop the mental wealth to be able to afford our dreams, and the mental strength to keep us on track. We just need to find the coaches and mentors to help us reach our potential.

Our minds are terrible things to waste. Please don't waste yours.

Author's Notes

My first childhood memory was living with my mother and brothers in a homeless shelter for battered women. As a teenager, I hung out with a tough group of friends and even owned a gun because it was expected of me. My path seemed predetermined—and then suddenly a friend was murdered and I did an about-face, using my self-will for the first time.

I began to build my mental strength and mental wealth, and I changed my life. I got a job, went to college, married my sweetheart, wrote a best-selling book, From the Hood to Doing Good, started my journey to wealth, and began speaking around the world. I coached, mentored, and founded philanthropies. As CEO and President of Wimbrey Training Systems, I oversee and create programs for personal development, wealth and career management, sales training, and speaker instruction.

I've also been a TV and radio host, and the co-author of several additional books, Multiple

Streams of Inspiration, Conversations on Success, Break Through, P.U.S.H. (Push Until Success Happens).

My newest solo book, Building a Millionaire Mindset, is being published at the end of 2020. In it, I focus on entrepreneurial success and lay out a simple "building block" approach to growing your business to the million-dollar level. Each chapter deals with a single task you must complete before you move on to the next one, and I share my insights and give you tools to help you make it happen.

My wife and best friend, Crystal, and I live a busy and fulfilling life in Southlake, Texas with our three wonderful children—our daughters Psalms and Hannah, and our son, Honor.

Contact Information

Johnny D. Wimbrey

Master Motivation/Success Trainer
Most Requested Topics:
Motivation/Keynote
Overcoming Adversity
Youth Enrichment
Leadership/Sales
www.JohnnyWimbrey.com

 @Wimbrey

 Wimbrey

 @Wimbrey

 JohnnyWimbrey

14

Chapter 2

The First Bill You Pay Is the One You Owe Yourself

Eric Cabrera

So, you have wants and desires. You're ready to take life to the next level. You might crave a new car, a house, more money, a loving spouse, or to improve an important relationship. Let me ask you: *What have you done to achieve these things?*

Now is the time to be honest with yourself.

Up until now, the chances are that you've acted like most of the people in the world, and you haven't seized the opportunity to better yourself, taken a chance on yourself, or stepped out of your comfort zone to grab what you desire. You haven't done so because, before you even took the first step, you counted yourself out.

You count yourself out because of a negative physical or emotional experience from your past. While you've dreamed of taking life to the next level, you don't have the hunger—and faith in yourself—to do it. Instead, your faith is in your own excuses and what other people say and think about you. You value other people's opinion of you more than you value yourself and your own capabilities. You don't entirely believe you deserve your heart's desire.

You have allowed your beliefs to create a false sense of fear.

So many of you are stuck in this identical cycle because of your past. You all have had challenges, obstacles, stories of loss, and failures in your lives, some that have continued for years and some that are very short-lived. Too many people are stuck because you don't love yourself enough to know your own true value.

> *Knowing your self-worth gives you the strength and confidence to choose opportunities to improve your life or someone else's and pass on those that won't.*

Too many of us don't fully recognize our self-worth.

Self-worth is a reflection of our overall vision of ourselves, built up over our lifetime, and always evolving. It's a combination of who we think we are, what we truly believe we deserve, and our faith in our own abilities. Self-worth is also affected by our innate belief system—for example, whether we automatically think and react positively or negatively.

16

When I was younger, I had no self-worth. I grew up in New York in a very dysfunctional household. During my childhood, being dragged out of bed and kicked around was routine for me. My mother loved me and was horrified by my father's abuse, but she was unable to protect me and in no position to leave the marriage. She had multiple sclerosis and breast cancer and was totally reliant on my father for support.

When I was eight years old, my father pushed me through a wall, breaking my collarbone and dislocating my shoulder. I remember holding back my tears, focusing my pain as energy to keep from crying because I knew if I cried, he beat me even harder.

As a young adult I recognized and overcame the effects of my childhood environment. I was able to recognize that my knee-jerk reactions impacted my relationships with others. For example, when my wife and I argued early in our marriage, any tears she might shed only made me angrier.

When I finally dug down enough to understand the trigger, I was so relieved: My anger at her tears was because I could never cry as a boy, no matter what abuse I suffered. That insight took years of hard work and awareness. I finally realized she had every right to cry, and I apologized for all the times I'd been mad.

But when I was still a boy, the years of childhood abuse just left me hating who I was and always feeling angry, scared, and alone.

Worst of all, I felt worthless. I truly believed I was.

On July 7, 1988, I was 12 years old. My father had just come home and I was rushing up the stairs to hide in my room and avoid him. He ordered me to come back downstairs, and I hesitated in terror of what might happen. As I turned around, he was rushing up the stairs, headed right at me. I crouched down to protect myself as he pounded me with his fists. When he was finally tired of punching, he kicked me down the flight of stairs and went to his bedroom.

When I managed to get to my feet, everything seemed to move in slow motion. My nose was bleeding and my body hurt all over. My mother was standing in front of me, crying and saying something, but I couldn't understand her through the ringing in my ears. I looked down the hallway into the kitchen, thinking *I can get a knife and kill him when he passes out, or I can walk out the front door and never come back.* Thank God, I chose to walk out the door. I left with nothing, not even shoes on my feet.

When I reflect on that pivotal moment, I now recognize I left that house with a lot more than just my bare feet. I left with a fresh start to a new life. I left with strength, dignity, courage, and self-respect. I left with a smidgen of self-worth. I left with all those things and didn't even know it at the time. It took years to figure out that I chose *me*!

I made the choice to change my life when I decided *I am worth more than this and I deserve a better life,* left home, and never returned. Other than staying in touch with my mother and brother, I severed all ties and was on my own as a teenager.

Life didn't suddenly take a sunny path, however, just because I left home. I spent the next five years angry and making bad choices, often homeless, hanging out in the wrong places, and surrounding myself with people who were going nowhere. I was headed to the exact same nowhere with them.

When I was 17, a terrifying experience I had while running drugs made me realize this was not the lifestyle for me. I knew I needed to get out of New York, so that night I bought a one-way plane ticket to Florida on the first flight out the next morning.

When I left New York with exactly $306 in my pocket, I had never been to Florida, didn't know anyone, and didn't have a place to stay. That didn't bother me, because I had been homeless off and on, and I knew Florida would at least be warmer than New York. On my first night in Orlando, I found a room to rent. A week later, I landed a job as a stock boy in a department store.

Soon after, while I was listening to an older gentleman who was telling me his life story (that guy loved to talk), I heard words that shook my soul to the core: *I can be a victim or a conqueror, but I love myself too much to be a victim, and I know my value. Do you know **yours**?*

Something inside me shifted. I knew my mindset wasn't that of a victim, but then I realized it definitely wasn't a conqueror's, either. Instead, it was stuck in the middle, in a no-man's-land. Plenty of my history could entitle me to play the victim card, but even at 17, I knew that's exactly what it was—just old history. It was behind me. I didn't need to be stuck anymore. My beatings were the result of my father's issues, not mine.

What happened wasn't my fault and I didn't need to bear the burden of his problems.

As time went on, I realized my responsibility is to love myself and know my self-worth, and that's a prerequisite for living a joyful life. My happiness is just that—*my* happiness—no one else's. After absorbing that bit of wisdom, I was able to figure out that my past doesn't dictate my future: *Where I've been doesn't control where I'm going.* I needed to start loving myself and learn my value and self-worth. I looked back at all of life's opportunities I had missed because I was just existing, not living. I was dead inside. I was blind and unable to see the greatness inside me because it was buried in the grave of darkness caused by the shadows of my past.

20   Years of hard work and self-improvement followed this initial insight.

You can learn from history's greatest people, including Abraham Lincoln, Albert Einstein, Martin Luther King Jr., and Thomas Jefferson, but some of the most valuable lessons in life will come from your own history.

Look at your history. Look at every failure, every loss, every setback, and I guarantee you can find a lesson. The lesson may not be *what to do* because *what not to do* can be equally valuable. When you look back, tell yourself you're thankful for these experiences because you will find positive lessons in them.

I promise you if you look for the positives, you will find them! This will allow you to look at each failure as a step closer to success, every loss as a gain, every setback as a catalyst to advancement.

Finding positive lessons helps you appreciate and celebrate those failures, losses, setbacks, and past events. This shifts your mind to start thinking positively, the first step to loving yourself enough to build your self-worth.

As your self-worth grows, as you develop a favorable opinion of yourself, you'll also start to build unshakeable faith in yourself. You are not a prisoner of your past or anyone else's. Look at your past as a lesson, not as a life sentence! You'll realize you don't have to live in the past and that you can live today with tomorrow in mind.

I'm in my early forties, retired from my first career, and living in Colorado. One morning my phone rang; it was my aunt calling to say my father had a stroke. I called the hospital and learned my father was on a ventilator, unable to breathe on his own because of brain damage. I got on a plane to see him; I felt it was the right thing to do.

I talked to him for the first time in more than 30 years, and I forgave him for everything that happened and for everything he did to me. I could forgive him because I love myself and I have a strong understanding of my self-worth. I am now able to find so many valuable lessons after many years of living scared, angry, sad, unloved, and feeling completely worthless. After I thanked him, he was taken off life support, and I held his hand until he took his last breath.

Because I know the value of my self-worth, I was able to handle my father's death in the way I did. My faith in myself doesn't depend on his or anyone else's

21

opinion. Your faith in yourself should be based on *your* opinion and yours alone.

I learned to change my mindset to match the desires of my heart by changing my outlook, and by speaking positively, not negatively. There is so much power in the spoken word. You should speak positively and as if the desires of your heart have already manifested. Set short-term and long-term goals. Set goals so high that it makes you feel uncomfortable saying them out loud. Set goals that most would see as unobtainable.

Everything that happens to you, your whole situation, is a product of what you believe. If things aren't working out, it is because you *believe* they won't. Your past has created such a fear inside of you that you don't believe in yourself. You are living your life to please others based on the fear of your past and what others think. Do not settle for a life based on fear.

Spend more time on yourself, and spend more time learning the value of your self-worth. You owe it to yourself, and that is the first bill you should pay. (Well, after you pay your mortgage, or you'll end up homeless!) You probably don't realize it, but you're financing a way of life, and you're using your happiness, your self-love, and your self-worth as collateral. Continue down this road and you'll end up broke and broken. When you truly believe and understand the value of your self-worth, you will be able to say *no* to those negative things that prevent you from achieving the God-given greatness that is inside you.

This is *your* story, *your* situation, nobody else's. Take a hard inventory of your strengths and weaknesses.

Identify your key strength. Build and train that strength not just until you get it right, do it until you can't get it wrong. Only then begin working on your weaknesses. Master your craft.

Who cares what other people think or say about you? They're going to think and say it anyway, and they probably already have. Don't sacrifice your greatness because of somebody else's doubts.

Be hungry! Hunger leads to happiness. Do not let anything stand in your way. Be willing to do whatever it takes, but humble enough to learn from others who inspire you and you want to emulate. Be confident in yourself, love yourself.

Self-improvement is limitless. It's a never-ending process and requires constant evaluation of yourself. Prepare yourself for the amazing opportunities life is going to bring you. It doesn't matter what your level of success is. It doesn't matter how big your house is or what kind of car you drive. You need to have a good understanding of who you are, what your purpose is, why you want that big house, that nice car, or that fat bank account. Your net worth is insignificant if you don't have significant self-worth!

Our lives are nothing but opportunities that present themselves in all shapes and sizes, and the size of our lives is limited by how we respond. When you meet someone, that's an opportunity to make a new friend. When a new job becomes available, that's an opportunity to make more money. When someone invites you to dinner, that's an opportunity to spend

23

time with a person you know. When a friend asks you to help them move, that's an opportunity to do good.

Knowing your self-worth gives you the strength and confidence to choose opportunities to improve your life or someone else's and pass on those that won't. The great civil rights leader Whitney M. Young Jr., said, "It is better to be prepared for an opportunity and not have one than to have an opportunity and not be prepared."

When I was finally able to look at my past from a positive perspective and started loving myself, I realized the value of my self-worth. This created powerful energy inside me, and I knew I deserved better for myself, for my future family, and for the community around me (because you always have to give). I had this insatiable hunger to learn and reach my goals of success because I knew I'm worth it! I told myself every day that I was worth it. My self-worth allowed me to accept opportunities without fear.

Not knowing the value of your self-worth will blind you from seeing and accepting great opportunities when they show up in your life. Not knowing your self-worth will allow you to degrade and discount yourself, saying *I can't do that* or *It won't work* rather than seizing the opportunity.

Let's look at it from a positive perspective. What if you *could* do it, and what if it *did* work? When I'm on my deathbed, I would rather be able to say *I'm glad I tried* or *I'm glad I did* instead of *I wish I would've tried*.

You are worth it! Take this opportunity to learn from your past by taking each negative experience and find a lesson in it. Take this opportunity to spend time on yourself, not on things that waste your time. Take this opportunity to invest in yourself by committing to self-improvement. Take this opportunity to make a plan, not excuses. Take this opportunity to set goals and have solid faith in your abilities to achieve them so you can set new and higher goals. Take this opportunity to start saying out loud every single day, *I am worth it, I have a high degree of self-worth, I am worthy of good things, and I love myself and who I am.*

Listen to yourself when you say those words.

I promise you, do these few things and your life will dramatically change. You *are* worth it.

Author's Notes

After I retired as a lieutenant with 23 years of distinguished service in the Fire Department, I moved to Colorado. I dedicate this project to my three sons, Liam, Riley, and Declan. You are my best friends, you are my "WHY." Love, Dad!

As a dedicated entrepreneur, I've built and sold several businesses. I'm also a real estate investor

and philanthropist, and serve on the executive board of two nonprofit organizations. Currently, I own two health club chains, and I'm in demand as a motivational speaker.

Contact information

Email:	Generalincrease@gmail.com
Website:	www.Generationalincrease.com
Instagram:	@the_eric_cabrera
Facebook:	Eric Cabrera
LinkedIn:	@eric-cabrera-9879201b9

Chapter 3

C-Notes: Currency to Build Your Mental Wealth

Tina Haskins Smith

Wealth is usually associated with finance because it's a game of deposits and withdrawals: The more money you withdraw from your bank account, the less wealthy you become. The more money that builds up in your bank account from your deposits, the wealthier you are.

A parallel theory applies to your mental wealth. The more you build and develop your *confidence, character, competency, connections*, and *community*, the more powerful your mental wealth becomes. I call these five concepts *C-notes*, which is also a term for hundred-dollar bills.

Confidence

With the combination of COVID-19, the economy's downward spiral, and the movement for justice can be overwhelming. Self-doubt can creep into our thinking: *Have I suppressed seeing the injustice that's going on around me? Have I missed speaking up when things were wrong? Have I provided the leadership my teams need since transitioning to a remote workplace?* It's easy to doubt yourself as a leader.

When self-doubts start knocking at my door, I don't let them in. Instead, I let in self-awareness, a far more positive emotion. The two are related, but affect us very differently. Self-doubt can deplete our mental wealth and our confidence. Self-awareness actively builds our confidence.

> *Confidence, character, competency, connections, and community... they are the C-notes—the hundred-dollar bills—that we use to build the balance of our mental wealth.*

Self-doubt is a stop sign—a hard stop that paralyzes your mental state. Self-awareness is a yield sign that slows you down while allowing you to continue moving ahead.

We are making withdrawals from our mental wealth if we're consistently paralyzed by self-doubt. We must transition from self-doubt to self-awareness, which allows us to recognize our fears and insecurities as we confidently move ahead to reach our goals.

Character

Emails, meetings, action items, projects . . . I feel the need to respond to everything that comes my way. My perfectionism always rises to the occasion and ensures I complete everything, but I become tired and can border on exhaustion.

We are making withdrawals from our mental wealth when we're always striving for perfection. People wrongly associate perfection with character. I've learned that imperfections build character, and as long as integrity is maintained, imperfection allows us to be more authentic and innovative.

Now I'm learning to pick three things from my never-ending pile to focus on and complete. I know I'm a better leader when I have a sense of accomplishment and I'm not being spread too thin. 29

One important meeting I will never cancel is the meeting I schedule with myself on a regular basis. I need time to clear my thoughts, spend time with family and friends, contact my doctors for my regular checkups, and exercise.

Competency

I am currently leading the implementation of an electronic healthcare record (EHR) system at the large medical system where I work. This is a sophisticated technology that will make work easier for clinicians providing care and service to our patients and families. I exhibit my competency in processes, project management, and technology while bringing over 10,000 people together for a common goal that represents a multi-million-dollar investment.

In the middle of an EHR implementation complicated by a pandemic, decisions are much tougher to make. Using data helps me to make decisions that keep everyone safe, but data alone is not enough. In addition to the facts, when I make my decisions, I use something that can't always be easily explained—and that is wisdom. Over time, we learn we don't have to have all the facts to make a decision. With wisdom, we use a compilation of facts, experience, and discernment to make good decisions. That is a definition of competency.

We are making withdrawals from our store of mental wealth if we think just being smart is enough. Anyone can have book knowledge, but we become mentally stronger when we complement the facts with wisdom. When we exercise discernment along with facts, our competency increases our mental bank account.

Connections

I recently reconnected with a senior executive I'd met at a healthcare industry conference. Our connection could have easily stopped there, but it has extended far beyond our friendship. As a CIO of a major pediatric organization, she knows many people in the medical IT field, and she sends me information about career opportunities. Being introduced to a wide variety of key decision-makers has increased my opportunities for advancement and given me more options. It's great to know her, and I appreciate how she looks out for my interests.

In addition to connecting to decision-makers, I also connect with younger people on their way up through mentoring. I mentor students at Texas A&M University's Mays Business School through AGGIEvisors and also serve as the mentor liaison for the Black and Heritage Network at the Seattle Children's Hospital.

Networking can be challenging for people, especially if you are an introvert. However, it is important to reach beyond our fears and personality to explore new connections. We should also make deposits in other's mental bank accounts by connecting them to people we know.

We are making withdrawals from our mental wealth assets if we think just knowing people is enough. Knowing people who introduce us to others enriches our mental deposits by creating far more options for opportunities and connections.

Community

My parents still live in Duncanville, a small suburban city close to both Dallas and Ft. Worth, Texas, where I grew up. It's a friendly community that molded me and invested in me, and it gave me good schools, good opportunities, and good friends. As part of my belief in the community and the future, I invest in STEM initiatives for youths in Duncanville. Healthcare technology is quickly evolving into emerging innovations and careers, and I want to help a new generation find a better path. Literacy is another cause close to my heart that I support.

Giving back to others makes deposits in my mental bank account. It also humbles me and gives me great hope for the future of our youth, as others did for me.

Now I live and work in Seattle, Washington. As in other major cities, gentrification has occurred and it's hard for lower-income people to find affordable housing and services. The Odessa Brown Children's Clinic, an inner-city facility, is near and dear to my heart; it offers mental health, wellness, and dental services as well as traditional medical programs. I have the honor of giving back to the clinic, not just financially through the Friends of Odessa Brown Children's Clinic Guild, but also through service by partnering with others to provide innovative technology solutions in the new Odessa Brown Children's Clinic.

I've been the recipient of many opportunities that progressed my career; it's important to me that I repay the blessings that came my way and in turn invest in the community in which I live. I'm always looking for organizations or causes to support financially, as well; most of them are in my areas of passion: technology, business, and healthcare. I want to help youth learn more about those fields.

I have been blessed to have two communities, both Duncanville and Seattle, and to be in a position to give back to both. We need to leave a legacy for the next generation. In many ways, serving others enriches our mental wealth and allows us to do even more. Blessings cannot stop with us. They must flow through us to others.

We are making withdrawals from our mental wealth resources if we think just our presence alone is enough of a gift to give to our community. We must invest in the place in which we live. We must leave a legacy in our community reflecting the depth of our mental wealth.

Conclusion

The year 2020 will never be forgotten. It has challenged us in unimaginable ways. In what seemed like an instant, the year stripped us of almost everything we have taken for granted . . . where we eat, what we do for entertainment, how we can gather, our options for learning, where we are allowed to go. Millions have lost their homes and their jobs. Too many have lost their lives.

2020 has tested the stability of our mental wealth. [33] All of us have probably had times when we felt mentally overdrawn. Our everyday lives have challenges we never dreamed of. We have established home offices to accommodate working from home. We have become teachers to our children. We have become short-order cooks for our families with snacks and meals around the clock.

However, through it all, we can find ways to build our mental wealth. The pandemic is revealing our imperfections, and each one gives us opportunities to excel. We're developing great character because we are showing we can thrive through tough times.

The stock market has highs and lows. We take for granted that our investments are easily affected by external forces and personal decisions about investments. One day the market is trending up, the next day, the market is heading down, and we're relatively philosophical about it. Most of us keep putting our money in whether it's a bull market or bear market, believing that in the long term, we'll come out far ahead.

Our mental wealth is built the same way our investment wealth in banks and the stock market is built. External forces and personal decisions definitely can affect our mental wealth. However, if we invest more positive deposits into our mental investment account instead of negative withdrawals, we will come out far richer in the long term.

Confidence, character, competency, connections, and community . . . they are the C-notes—the hundred-dollar bills—that we use to build the balance of our mental wealth.

Author's Notes

As a philanthropist and IT executive, I credit my parents, Thomas and Barbara Haskins, for teaching me the importance of work and education along with the value of faith, family, and fun. My experiences in Virginia, Texas, Pennsylvania, New York, Washington, and Spain have contributed to my servant leadership style.

Giving to others is a natural part of my life, and I support a wide variety of organizations, including Black Girls CODE, Dignity for Divas, Metropolitan Seattle Sickle Cell Task Force, The Links, Beacon Hill Preparatory Institute, Housing Solutions for Hope Guild, Friends of Odessa Brown Children's Clinic Guild, and Seattle Children's Research Institute. I'm a proud member of Delta Sigma Theta, Incorporated, and served on the board of Texas HOPE Literacy, Inc., when I lived in Texas.

My degrees are a B.B.A. in Business Analysis (Management Information Systems) from Texas A&M University, and an M.B.A. in Management from Amberton University. My additional specialized training includes the CHIME Healthcare CIO Boot Camp and Harvard School of Public Health–Leadership

35

Strategies for Information Technology in Health Care.

Past positions have included stints as Assistant Vice President, Program Management Office Director, and ITIL Service Delivery Manager with a Project Management Professional Certification and ITIL v3 Foundation Certification. I've worked in a variety of industries and organizations, including American Airlines, IBM, First American/Transamerica Real Estate Tax Service, Parkland Health & Hospital System, and Cook Children's Health Care System.

Now a Seattle resident, I'm the Senior IT Director of Enterprise Clinical Systems and Epic Project Director at Seattle Children's Hospital. I start my days with devotional time and a workout, and listen to podcasts and read books to continue to learn and grow. I love hanging out with my sister and my long-term friends, and dote on my nephews and nieces, receiving the "Aunt of the Year" award from them every year.

While 2020 has seen unprecedented darkness and trouble, I look forward to a lifetime of service, happiness, and mental wealth.

Contact Information:

Email: Tina.Haskins.Smith@gmail.com
LinkedIn: @TinaHaskinsSmith

Chapter 4

Diving In Head First

Thressa M. Stehr

*She's only successful because
she is tall, pretty, and skinny.
She probably came from money
and was given everything.*

Have you ever been stereotyped? I was. People said these things behind my back for years, but they're far from the truth. My life has never been rainbows and unicorns.

I was raised by my single mom and grandparents until I was four. My stepdad came in the picture around that time. At first, I was thrilled because I had never met my biological father. Having a dad in the house was exciting, right up until it wasn't. The reality was not at all like my image of a live-in daddy. We never managed to communicate well, and we had an unhealthy relationship, especially in the way it affected me. In fact, I felt like it came between the relationship I had with my mom, and suddenly I was not as important to her.

Things deteriorated when I was seven and we moved to a town 45 minutes away from my grandparents. It was especially difficult to be away from my grandmother, Mimi, who'd made me feel safe from the moment I was born. From that point on, I felt profoundly rejected and unwanted at home. I never felt good enough; I never measured up as the "perfect child" my stepfather expected and demanded. Instead, I heard over and over, "You will never do anything productive in life," and "Stop trying to be someone that you're not." I began to rebel more openly.

You own the key to unlock your success—grab it, take action, and don't allow anyone to tell you otherwise.

I begged for a sister, and my wish came true when I was nine. When my sister Karmin was born, I was happy to help take care of her and play mamma. As she grew older, though, I became the one with primary responsibility for her care because my parents were busy earning our living. I'd always loved and played multiple sports but my new responsibilities kept me from participating as much as I wanted. My resentment grew.

My angel, my Mimi, prayed for me day and night. She was the constant in my life. We had a very special relationship and I told her everything. She believed in me and I believe that's why God had His hand on me and I was protected. Even though I was rebellious and made bad decisions sometimes, He always protected me. Even as I reached middle school and my childhood became unbearable, I've known God had plans for me to have more in life

Years later, as I became older and wiser and looked back at my time of pain and turmoil, I realized I'd done my part to make it hard on my stepfather. When I reached that level of maturity and understanding, I did my best to improve our relationship so he would accept me as I am. Forgiveness is key and can heal a broken road. The day I was married, I was happy for my stepfather to fill the role of father, and he proudly walked me down the aisle.

But when I was 12 years old, long before my stepfather and I reached our understanding, it seemed impossible that we'd ever get along. I ran away after we had a massive argument, a move that really backfired on me because it became even harder to have a good relationship with him or my mother. I managed to hold on for five more years.

A month after I started my senior year, I ran away again from home a second (and final) time after another major argument with my parents. Everything always seemed to be my fault, and I could never live up to their expectations. I felt so unwanted, I told them I would no longer be a burden and left. My parents did not speak to me for the rest of the school year unless it was about something that needed to be signed for school.

Though I knew leaving was hurtful to my mom, I couldn't bear all the fighting we had at home. Being on my own and homeless was hard, but it was still easier than the conflict.

This time my exit was a success because I was determined I was going to go do *more* in life. I was always searching for *more*. I never knew *what* exactly but I knew I wanted MORE!

For the next five months, I lived with my best friend and her parents. I shared my friend's twin-size waterbed, and her father gave me $20 each week for lunch money at school. Though I was already working at Office Max, I started a second job as a server at IHOP because I knew it was time to be an adult and work nonstop. I needed to make money and I was willing to do whatever it would take. I wanted to accomplish what my stepdad thought I could never do.

For the final three months of my senior year, I lived with my grandparents. I worked hard and was so determined to succeed that I graduated with my highest grades ever. As soon as I reached the legal age of 18, I moved out and rented my first apartment.

From the moment I left home, I worked hard and held multiple jobs. I went into the automotive business, some mentors took me under their wings, and soon I became a sales manager in the aftermarket department. After four years, when I was only 22, I bought my first house, and I was *so* proud. I made good money working and traveling as Midwest regional sales manager for a company that made navigation and DVD systems for vehicles. I loved the travel and work, but because I always had a couple of side jobs, I didn't have a moment for myself. As a young woman in her twenties, I had absolutely no social life.

Suddenly, the 2008 Great Recession hit, and I found myself without my supposedly secure six-figure income. There I was, a single 26-year-old woman and the only female sales manager, and they let me go and kept the two men. I was scared, shocked, empty, and confused. To my surprise, I was also burned out.

Much later, I realized one of the main reasons I was so exhausted and empty at such a young age was because of the demands of one of my side jobs. Just a year before, I'd earned my massage therapy license. Because I love helping others, it seemed it'd be a perfect fit as a part-time, flexible job. Little did I know at the time that I wore a neon sign on my forehead: *Please share your life story with me and I will counsel you.*

I'm not sure why people immediately can tell I have great empathy toward others and a desire to help people better themselves, but they sure do. The hours of counseling became exhausting and draining. After five years of massage therapy with a free serving of life coaching/counseling on the side, I gave up my license.

But four years before I finally reached that point, at the moment when I lost my traveling sales job and my big-ticket income, I asked myself, *NOW what?*

My fear didn't last long. Losing my main income turned out to be perfect timing. For three years, I'd been involved with network marketing as one of my multiple side gigs but hadn't done much with it. Finally, I had the time and incentive to dive in headfirst, which is the only way I really know how to do anything. As I rediscovered my love of truly helping others, I remembered that was why I wanted to be a nurse when I was growing up.

After almost ten years out on my own, believing I was all grown up, finally, I *was* an adult and ready to take a second headfirst jump—into personal development. I'd always thought I just had to work harder and longer than anyone else to succeed. Now I understand personal development is a key part of anyone's true, ongoing success. The process is never finished; personal development needs to be worked on throughout our lives.

In 2009, when I was 27 years old, I was chosen to be one of six women on a national television documentary on American Life Network: *RAW: Revelations of Authentic Women.* The format was a new concept called "talkumentary," a talk-show series about successful women taking off their masks and revealing their true struggles and insecurities. We used video journaling and mentoring to help with healing from trauma.

The processes we went through during the filming revealed some truths that I had not yet faced: A full ten years after I left home, I still hadn't recovered from my intense feelings of rejection, and I hadn't begun to overcome what I call "daddy issues." I began to think there was something wrong with me. When a man would get close to me, whenever we had any type of conflict I would push him away so he could not "leave" me. I had to dig deep, find forgiveness, and realize that there was nothing wrong with me. I just yearned for love!

My abandonment/rejection issues had been compounded when I'd had the opportunity to meet my biological father five years earlier. When he told me he did not want a relationship with me and he thought I was not his daughter, I was torn. A part of me was crushed that he rejected me, and then another part knew that *he* was the one missing out. After meeting him, I felt like I had some closure.

During one of the *RAW* episodes, each of us was given a glass plate. We wrote onto our plate the burden we no longer wanted to continue carrying through life, then we took hammers and smashed our plates into tiny shards of glass. I wrote down "feeling abandoned and rejected by my father and stepfather," and the symbolic act of shattering those words was so invigorating and freeing!

The documentary became a journey and a time of growth. I grew, I forgave, and I lifted a weight off myself that I no longer carry.

By the end, I became whole within, and at that point, I knew I had more to give. I could help those who struggled with rejection, abandonment, and not being able to feel enough. God is so good. He wove a broken girl into a strong woman with a plan and a purpose to help empower others to be all they were created to be.

It turns out I had strengths I never realized I'd had or had never worked on. As I learned how to communicate more skillfully, build my team, and then in turn teach my team to build their own teams, I discovered that teaching and coaching were also my passions.

While I love building others up, my tolerance is limited. I don't put up with laziness or excuse-makers,

43

and I teach my team: *Own it! Take responsibility and put your actions behind it!*

The journaling I did during that television documentary, both in videos and in writing, taught me the value of capturing my thoughts and plans in my own words and reviewing them. I believe journaling will help you as well.

Let's look at some concepts and thoughts you can include in your journal. I ask my team to periodically ask themselves, "What is my purpose?" and it helps to put the answer in writing.

Do you write down your desires in life? Do you have a plan? Is your worth attached to what you hope to accomplish? What are the concepts you repeat to yourself daily? Are you living to your full potential?

Let's work on uprooting bad habits and importing new habits. I want to help you live a life by design, one that's lived on purpose and not by default. Let's make sure you have a clear vision and a dream for your life. What does your best life look like?

Let's establish some daily routines and take action. We can create small wins that will turn into big wins. We will work on creating a life of intention. We will work on daily affirmations that will feed your body, soul, and mind. Let's live an abundant life by design. Let's learn to live out loud!

If you're not learning, you're not growing.

We all have a story. We all have been tested by life to some degree, and our tests are meant to be a testimony so we can help others. We are all enough in God's eyes and we all have a purpose. Loving yourself is the best gift you can give *you*!

To truly have a full, satisfying, successful life, you need to do things you love and enjoy.

What brings you JOY?

What makes you smile?

What's so cool about life is the chapter that we continue to write. Everything in life comes full circle. Broken roads can be mended. No matter where you are on your journey, just know there is a plan for your life. You were meant for more!

When I decided *I* was meant for more and jumped headfirst (as usual!) into the direct sales/network marketing world, I jumped into the so-called "Pink Bubble," aka Mary Kay. I went fast and furious and reached the top two percent worldwide during my first six months. I earned five cars during my ten years as a sales director. *Yes,* I *did* drive the pink Cadillac!

Though I helped thousands of women gain their confidence and their own voice, after a decade I realized *I* had stopped growing and was yearning for more. When I was introduced to a health and wellness company, I again did my usual headfirst dive, fully committed to my new role.

Good changes happened immediately. Not only did the company's products improve my family's health, but they also elevated my leadership skills and I earned in the high six-figure range in my first year. My team grew extremely fast, and we have more than 2,500 people helping others find their best, most complete health.

What I learned through the years is that *your alignments determine your assignments.* I've been introduced to some very well-known and high-level leaders who have what I need and who took me down another road to learning, growing, and helping others be more empowered.

I am blessed to be in the arena of visionary leaders who have created an environment of excellence. This is just the beginning of greater things to come.

I look forward to helping you grow and evolve into a person with passion and purpose. You can be *anything* you want to be, you can do *anything* you want to do, as long as you are willing to pay the price. I would be happy to be there by your side.

Author's Notes

Because I am extremely particular about my negotiables and non-negotiables in a relationship, I waited until later in life to settle down. It was important to me that my husband would be the best husband and dad ever. Chris and I married in 2016 and have a beautiful daughter, Ruby Love, who will soon be three.

It brings me great joy to be close to my mother and stepfather and part of an extended family. My daughter, my stepdad, and my mom have a wonderful relationship—the one I always wanted to have with them, and I share it through her love.

When my stepfather came into my life, I gained a bonus big brother, Brandon, just a year older than I am. He and I saw each other on weekends and in the summertime, but we never were really close until we became adults. He and his beautiful family now live only 15 minutes from me and we visit often.

My half-sister Karmin was born when I was nine, and I felt like a little mamma to her. She is now grown up with a beautiful seven-year-old daughter. When I met my biological father, I learned I had another half-sister, Baylee, 14 years younger. She attends law school, and we're in touch.

47

Chris and I live in both Texas and Oklahoma, and we are serial entrepreneurs.

Contact information

Email: Twaller242000@yahoo.com
Website: www.thressastehr.com
Facebook: Thressa.waller
Facebook: thressastehr
Twitter: @twaller24
Instagram: @twaller24

Chapter 5

Use Every One of Your Six Senses

Tony Bryant

Growing up, my mental focus was simple: avoid pain and loneliness, stay away from negativity, hang with positive people, and never settle for being average.

I grew up in Crosby, Texas, a little town outside of Houston. Children in my low-income apartment complex were never expected to achieve more than the bare minimum life had to offer—get minimum wage jobs and survive with the help of charitable groups or welfare. Even as a child, I knew my life was *not* going to travel that path. I had ambition; I was different. I was determined to discover the way to become successful rather than become just another statistic.

My mission was to achieve more mental and monetary success than anyone I had met to that point in my life. My fear of ending up dead, in jail, broke, or unmotivated, bragging about my crowning achievements in high school athletics, would come to fruition if I didn't come up with a plan.

In my most vulnerable moments, when I knew I was in over my head, I was convinced I had to fake it until I could make it. Somehow, stretching the truth felt necessary to be part of the in-crowd. When I exaggerated, I had temporary protection from the hurtful comments of other kids and the confidence that came from feeling I had as much money and support as my peers.

Think things through; go after whatever you believe you're capable of doing and don't rest until you reach your destination.

Growing up as a teen in the materialistic 90s was tough. I enviously watched my peers strut through what seemed to be daily fashion shows. To my eyes, they had fresh gear and the latest pair of Air Jordans for each day of the week. I was all too aware that I wore my brother's hand-me-downs and got Wal-Mart shoes twice a year. When I was asked about my clothes, sometimes I managed to put my chin up and say, "My value isn't in what I choose to wear." Sometimes, though, I'd lie, mumble something along the lines of, "My dad is getting even newer Air Jordans for me soon," and quickly change the subject.

I knew I was telling a boldfaced untruth as those words flowed out of my mouth. My parents divorced when I was nine. My mother was a wonderful mother, and I am so grateful to her; she has the biggest heart of anyone I know. I never saw my dad contribute one penny to our household. No shoes, clothes, or anything else was ever on its way or going to come on any later date from my dad.

Not too long ago, I asked my dad why things happened the way they did, and he simply said, "I was sick." He meant his addictions; his life was focused on crack cocaine and women. Those addictions caused him to lose his decent-paying job in the chemical plants, his marriage to my mother, and his relationship with my siblings and me.

Ironically, the Air Jordans I yearned for ended up being worth less over time than what I was able to buy in those days—some Michael Jordan basketball cards. I've hung onto those cards my entire life. Somehow, my son Maddox recently managed to find them and barter a few for Pokémon cards. By accident, my childhood hobby of basketball cards turned out to be a great first investment.

51

As a teen, I was determined to not be lazy, get involved with drugs, participate in unnecessary drama, or settle for a dead-end job. In those days, I could have been granted access to anything negative my immature mind could imagine or desire. I could have easily been involved in quick illegal cash deals involving crime, sex, or drugs. I was not naive to the consequences. I had a front-row seat as I witnessed classmates, neighbors, my mother's boyfriend, and some of my own family members be locked up or die because of their addictions and desire to make a quick buck. Life was a struggle, but I managed to hold on to my thoughts and maintain mental control.

What was key to my survival was learning to see beyond what was right in front of me. My immediate environment gave me limited vision, and my mission was to change that, even though I didn't yet have a plan. I needed to remain optimistic in the toughest of situations. In every way, I needed to subconsciously stay awake and consciously change my dynamics. I had to develop focus and practice becoming mentally strong.

We are all capable of changing our circumstances by changing what we choose to believe. Along with having a huge amount of faith, the more we improve the quality of what we see, hear, and read eventually self-manifests. Obstacles become bumps in the road, just a natural part of our mission. I had to create a strategy to use every one of my senses to create my new reality. It was critical that wanting a better life forced me to raise my standards. I had the desire and will to change the field of life that I played on. I had to create my vision by using what God gave me.

The brain has a variety of inputs, and I used all of them, working with every one of my senses.

Sight: I created a detailed and specific vision of what my life would look like—what I was going to own, how it looked including the exact colors, the people around me, the amount of money I would have, and all the success I was to achieve.

Touch: Visiting car dealerships and sitting in new models, driving through desirable neighborhoods, and attending open houses became part of my weekly routine. I called it dream building. It all prepared me for what my life would feel like once I reached that level.

Hear: Most of what I read, spoke about, and heard had to fuel my growth. Everyone I associated with had to speak positively, not negatively—at work, at home, with friends, or anyone with whom I affiliated myself.

Taste: Occasionally, I would stretch my budget to eat at some of the finer restaurants in Houston. I wanted to know what it was like to enjoy quail, steak, and lobster served in beautiful surroundings by an impeccably professional waitstaff.

Smell: The luscious aromas of new houses, cars, and fine restaurants were going to be part of my daily life. I needed to know what those things smelled like.

Intuition: This bonus sense allowed me to make quick decisions, ones I didn't double-guess and that gave me confidence. In a way, my intuition navigated me to the realization of my dreams.

Once I was out on my own, I imagined the places I lived not as a scruffy apartment, but as a large and well-appointed home. I was not crazy or disillusioned, I just saw things in a different way than most people did. I filtered my vision to delete the poverty. I was hungry to achieve a better life and future. My mental wealth had to exist before my physical wealth ever could. I viewed my Pontiac Grand Am as though it were a high-end Mercedes, and I treated it that way, too.

Yes, I knew the journey would shed a few friends, and some people would believe I thought I was better than they were, especially those who shared my background. I was ready to create the person I was to become. I was ready to lose whatever I'd already attained to gain a more positive, productive, and secure future.

Once we discover that literally, any dream is possible to achieve, our confidence matures. We then eliminate the fear of taking action, and great things can happen.

I started planning for my future while I was still in high school, dedicating my weekends to working and church. I became the head banquet waiter at the local country club. Not only did I make decent money, but I was also able to glean life tips and special bits of wisdom from the older white members who played golf and lived in what I then considered mansions.

As a disadvantaged teenager, I developed the skill of learning from watching the actions, successes, and failures of other people. This skill has helped me to avoid many costly mistakes and losses as I grew older. I began to understand the value of positioning, leadership, consistency, word articulation, how to self-motivate, and many equally relevant skills.

On Sundays, I spent long hours in a Southern Baptist church, often from morning until late evening, avoiding the desperate lives at my apartment complex and attempting to disassociate myself from an impoverished mentality. Selfishly, after hours in church, I sometimes fell asleep when I was supposed to be worshiping. Even asleep, my time in the church significantly reduced the possibility of me being around the wrong crowds or getting into trouble.

I attribute my dogmatic mindset and achievements to my hours in church, staying consistently focused, praying, having vision and faith, and working hard.

By the time I was in my mid-twenties, I had put myself through college, held several leadership roles in sales and marketing management, did several real estate deals, experienced multiple business start-ups— and had many failures. I had also gained an impeccable work ethic, expert-level negotiating skills, and was sharp at financial and operational analysis. I was also more optimistic and had some confidence in taking on new opportunities and risks.

While I knew I still had a lot to learn, I was on top of the world and felt excitement like I had never felt before. I'd known this time would come because I had manifested it several years earlier.

The more friends I made, the more opportunities I was offered, and most times, I believed I had to be a part of these deals even when they weren't the best investments. I went into them with my heart, not my brain—and in every case, I was sure the potential to make profits existed because we shared honest intentions and similar work ethics.

Over time, I discovered I didn't always pick the right partnerships. In fact, I was dead wrong in many cases, even the so-called lucrative opportunities, because my heart consistently made the wrong decisions. Experiencing so many losses took a toll on my ego, stress level, and confidence as an investor.

The year 2008 was tough for me, financially and emotionally. In addition to my investment losses, and thanks to a reduction of 2,000-plus employees at my Fortune 500 company, my high-level career as a sales and marketing director was eliminated. Talk about adding fuel to a bonfire!

In my career, I'd already reached certain levels of success when it came to income, my role, and the impact I made. My bank account was healthy thanks to my company's payout, plus earlier real estate deals. However, none of that mattered to me because I'd always defined myself by my career; my entire identity was wrapped up in who I was at work and the role I played for an entity in which I had no ownership.

For all these years, I'd based my self-worth and value on what I chose to do for other people and not for myself. Now, for the first time in my life, I felt mentally stressed, even depressed. I had to find a way to snap out of it and rediscover my mental peace and confident performance.

I decided I was no longer going to be an employee. I never again wanted to put my energy into playing the corporate politics game or allow someone else to control my destiny. I decided to become a fulltime investor and entrepreneur. I also knew I also needed to avoid any potential investment that was barely good enough or that wasn't going to succeed. I had to put my mind back to work, not just my heart.

I was only able to do this with the full support of my lovely wife, Heather. She believed in me at times more than I believed in myself; she is my true rock and keeps me going. At that moment, I took the step that she had encouraged me to take several years earlier: I became my very own boss.

My first decision came after several months of self-evaluation and planning: We built on Heather's special talents as a dentist and opened a private dental practice. We also invested in more real estate, but only opportunities that we strongly believed in, and started several companies. At that point, I made the decision to continue to bet on and believe in myself, regardless of the situations I may face.

Twelve years after losing my job and my confidence, Heather and I own and operate a wide variety of successful businesses: dental practices, restaurant investments, trucking, a real estate investment firm, a private lending business, plus other opportunities. They all create generational wealth and allow us to add value to as many people as we can.

Success comes from our mind however we choose to define it. It cannot be achieved without a healthy, confident mind. Most of us tend to prioritize other people, things, or careers above ourselves and what we truly need to survive mentally. If we aren't strong mentally, we limit our capabilities to visualize and deliver physically.

Being mentally healthy plays a very important role in how we interact with others, execute opportunities, and live our daily lives. Just as our bodies need proper nutrients, our brain needs to be free of stress. Exercising daily, listening to calming music, spending time in nature, reading, having interactive conversations, and eliminating unnecessary tasks, are all things that add to the valuable growth of our mental abilities and health.

We need to do all we can to eliminate the small, irritating tasks and thoughts that don't give our lives added value. Worrying about competition, chasing fame and money, and fretting about our achievements weigh us down with huge amounts of pressure.

We aren't designed to withstand so much prolonged mental pressure. It's important to recognize we are human beings and none of us are invincible or immune to mental illness or breakdown. Do everything possible to remain mentally strong and healthy. Be responsible to yourself and take the lead position in your own growth. Life is too short to worry about things out of our control. Think things through; go after whatever you believe you're capable of doing and don't rest until you reach your destination.

I hope my humble start in life helps convince you that regardless of our backgrounds, anything is possible and we can all have strong, determined minds. We are in control of our own destinies. Life can always get better, and our best days are yet to come.

58

Author's Notes

Although I was born in Houston, I grew up in the nearby small town of Crosby, Texas. During my teen years, I lived with my mother and three siblings in a Section 8 low-income apartment complex. With a mainly absentee father and no mentors, role models, or clear direction, I did not know what I wanted to do with my life or what career choice to make. Instead, I knew exactly what I did not want out of life, and I did my best to avoid negative peer pressure, crime, and drugs.

By practicing mental discipline, I have become very successful—a millionaire by my late twenties. After serving in leadership roles in two major public companies, I left the corporate world and began my journey as a full-time entrepreneur in 2008.

I serve as the Chief Executive Officer of Home Buyers Texas LLC, a Houston-based real estate investment firm that focuses on adding value, empowering people, and improving communities. I also own and operate several other successful companies in multiple industries generating in excess of one million dollars in annual revenue: business consulting (financial/operational analysis), healthcare (dentistry), transportation (trucking), entertainment (contracts), restaurant/bars, investment education, private lending, and technology investments.

My commitment to lifelong education includes a BA in Management and MBA from the University of Phoenix, certificates in Leadership and Financial Management from the University of Houston, a Texas real estate license, and a private pilot's license.

My wife, Heather, and I live in Houston with our two daughters and two sons: Aubrey, Zarah, Maddox, and Caden.

Contact Information

Email:	TonyB.Interest@gmail.com
Website:	www.tonyb4profits.com
Facebook:	Tony Bryant
Instagram:	@tonyb4profits
Twitter:	@tonyb4profits

Chapter 6

Listen With Confidence

Heather Monahan

I have trained myself to listen. I'm not saying listening is easy or that it comes naturally to me; it definitely does not. I've trained myself to listen because I've learned a powerful fact: When people feel they are really and truly heard, the dopamine in their brain activates and they begin to feel happier. When people feel cheerful, they are more likely to work in harmony to find a solution.

Listening also signals respect, and respect can mean everything to some people.

A couple of years ago, I was called into a meeting at my son's school to address an issue with his behavior. While meetings like these are never fun, they have taught me a tremendous amount about dealing with adversity and growing as a person.

When you walk into a meeting, especially one that might become adversarial, it's easy to let your emotions get the better of you. There is no place for emotion in meetings; the one who shows emotion is the one who loses. I work to calm my breathing and focus on my strategy.

My strategy is to always let the other party "empty their cup" first. Once you do this, you have information to work from, and information empowers you. Heading into a meeting with your guns blazing or your mind filled with assumptions will leave you upset in the end. Very rarely will be you happy with the outcome.

" *There is no place for emotion in meetings; the one who shows emotion is the one who loses.*

I calmed myself, sat down, and did not speak.

Remaining calm and not speaking is not easy. It takes practice and discipline, but when you have a goal in mind, employing the right strategy is key to yielding the result you want. I let the school officials share their position, give me their opinions, and talk as much as they wanted to. People like to hear themselves talk. That is a fact of life. Let them. Let them feel heard. Gain information and position yourself to be empowered; it works every single time.

I could sense my cheeks getting hot. At this point in my life, very rarely do I allow myself to get emotional, with the sole exception of issues around my son, Dylan.

The people in our lives who mean the most to us always have the power to put us in very emotional states in trying times. I forced myself to remain calm and quiet.

Starting the meeting by absorbing all the information the other party has to share puts you in a position of power. I recommend this approach whenever you are walking into a difficult negotiation or meeting. When you enter a similar meeting where there is a potential challenge or disagreement, set yourself up for success by encouraging them to talk by asking them for their thoughts or opinions. Repeat back some of what they say; it helps to keep communication clear and let them know you have been actively listening. Don't say, "I hear you," though, because it does not mean you're listening. It's just an acknowledgment, and the phrase is trite and over-used.

At my school meeting, I listened with courtesy, with confidence, without defensiveness, and with encouraging questions. When they were finished, I was ready to begin.

My goal for this meeting was to ensure my son would be set up for success after I left the office that day. Now that I had heard their position, I was able to clearly see the path for me to achieve my goal. There are a number of ways to arrive at that outcome. It is up to us to see the dots and connect them in the best way possible. I saw the dots, and as I began speaking and asking follow-up questions, I began connecting them. Prior to walking into that meeting, I didn't know exactly what the solution would be, but I did know we could find one.

I started with the first observation from one of the teachers, that Dylan had responded aggressively to a specific situation while he was in her class. What struck me as odd was the teachers hadn't discussed or even alluded to the original situation that ignited this chain reaction with my son. *I* knew what the situation was because I had talked with my son in preparation for this meeting.

That looked like a good dot to connect, so I said something to the effect of, "When we began this conversation today, you started with an example of my son acting aggressively. Can you tell me, in your opinion, what elicited that reaction?"

I was confident and relaxed, because I already knew the answer, and asking her the question forced her to own the facts. Asking questions is an extremely powerful tactic. Asking questions you already know the answer to is an even more powerful tactic. The teacher explained that another boy had said something very cruel about my son on a public school forum.

Asking follow-up questions is a powerful course of action, so I said calmly, "Can we please pause for a moment, because I want to point out that *I'd* feel very angry if a peer of mine did that. Is that behavior allowed at school?".

Of course, mean-spirited behavior is not allowed at school, and she agreed that it was an issue. Next, I asked, "How do you think Dylan could have handled it better?"

"He should have called a teacher for help," she said.

That was my opening. Using an opportunity to gain knowledge and then finding ways to have the other person share their opinions allows you to connect the dots.

My logical follow-up question was, "How often *do* fifth-grade boys tell the teacher on each other?"

His teacher admitted, "I don't see that happen often, but I really wish that kids would tell me instead of handling it themselves." That gave me the opportunity to share information with her that she didn't know.

I explained, "We've worked with Dylan to learn to stand up for himself so that he's equipped to handle problems when there isn't a teacher or adult around. It's a strategy that we've worked on for a year. We all know that as we grow, our strategies and abilities evolve and develop. In theory, some things may work, but in reality often different and more realistic tactics or strategies are needed."

The teachers knew I had listened to them with respect, and they listened to me in turn. There wasn't a hint of adversarial attitude or negativity, and we all showed some empathy.

The meeting went on for an hour. We went back and forth between hearing how the school wanted things to be vs. putting ourselves in my son's shoes and discussing what is more realistic.

In the end, we all left the meeting feeling as though my son's motives and actions were now fully understood. So much good can come from being listened to and understood!

Listening signals respect, and it changes the atmosphere in the room. Especially if the others are criticizing you, *listen*. Don't be defensive—just listen. When I said my cheeks were getting hot in my school meeting, they were flaming. My son was being criticized—and by extension, that included me. I sat and listened with respectful confidence, not defensiveness. When it was my turn to talk, the first thing out of my mouth was a question, not a defensive statement. I handled the criticism well by not responding to it and diverted the conversation to problem-solving.

How you deal with criticism is very important, and it leads to a long-term benefit: Handling criticism well will boost your confidence in the long run—and *that's* a game-changer. Confidence is the one thing that changes everything in the environment. When you listen with confidence, you can embrace collaboration and contribute your own ideas.

I wrote the best-selling book, *Confidence Creator,* to share what I've learned on the subject. As a young woman in a male-dominated part of the corporate world, I had to develop confidence quickly to survive, much less thrive.

A good part of my life is now spent helping other people learn confidence. Yes, it can be learned. Building confidence is exactly like training a muscle that can be built up or depleted; it just depends on the actions you take. You always either build your confidence or chip away at it with every action you take. Once you realize that building confidence in yourself is not only attainable but entirely up to you, you're empowered.

You have this.

So, let's take a more confident look at a situation you're dealing with right now, something that isn't going the way you want.

Is it on the wrong track because everyone involved doesn't fully understand the situation?

Is it because *you* don't have enough information?

Listen with confidence. Don't be defensive. Gain the knowledge and insight you need.

Only then, *after* you've listened and asked questions, confidently share your perspective and opinion.

You will find a way to agree on a solution.

There is *always* a solution. It's just up to us to find it.

Author's Notes

As the founder and CEO of Boss in Heels, I am an entrepreneur. I'm also well-known as a confidence expert, keynote and TEDx speaker, and a best-selling author. My recent book, Confidence Creator, shot to number one on Amazon's Business Biography and Business Motivation best-seller lists the first week it was published.

I earned a B.A. in Psychology at Clark University in Worcester, Massachusetts, and began my career as a brand manager at Gallo Wine before I transitioned into broadcasting. After successfully climbing the corporate ladder for nearly 20 years, I was appointed Chief Revenue Officer for Beasley Media Group and was named one of the Most Influential Women in Radio in 2017.

After 14 years of success and continuous advancement, I was unexpectedly fired by another woman. That was one of my lowest moments and forced me to re-evaluate where I was gaining my confidence from. As I began to reflect, I realized that if I was going to start over as a rookie somewhere, I was going to double down on myself. That is when I made the decision to write and self-publish my first book, *Confidence Creator*, and go to work for myself. In 2018, I was named a Limit Breaking Female Founder by Thrive Global. Next, I launched my podcast *Creating Confidence* and landed on the Apple Podcast top 200 list. Then I was named a Top 40 Female Speaker in 2020 by Real Leaders. Today, my clients include Fortune 500 Companies and professional sports franchises, and I help their employees and clients develop confidence in the workplace and on the court.

I'm also very active in my southern Florida community. I was given the honor of receiving the 2015 Glass Ceiling Award from the Florida Women's Conference, recognizing my leadership excellence in the workplace. I'm also a member of Florida International University's Advisory Council, serving as a mentor and leader in the South Florida Community.

My son, Dylan, and I live in Miami.

Contact information

Website: heathermonahan.com
Facebook: Heather Monahan Official
Instagram: @Heather Monahan
Twitter: @_heathermonahan

Chapter 7

See It, Be It, Feel It

Edith Rajna

F ive thousand people were waiting to hear me speak in Dublin, Ireland, as I stood at the bottom of the stairs to the stage, listening for my name. I smoothed my hair, careful not to touch the microphone taped to my cheek, and prayed, "God, I am yours, please help me share the messages you wish of me so that those who need to hear you will receive you through me." Then I heard my name, stood tall, channeled my inner goddess, and went up the stairs.

This was the first time I'd spoken at an international conference. The front rows were full of my company's leaders, including many of my favorite speakers. Now that I had the honor to be on stage, I made sure to channel some of their inspiration and stage presence in my own unique way as I shared my passion in front of thousands.

I am an international volunteer, and my worldwide travels include more than two dozen mission trips. With the foundation I endowed, I have built three eco-bottle schools in Guatemala, a pediatric clinic in Cuzco, Peru, remodeled orphanages in Hungary and the Czech Republic, and completed many more projects.

During my speech I shared pictures and memories of these projects and described the impact we made in those communities, honoring the thousands of other volunteers who also participated in making those dreams a reality. I am extremely grateful to be a part of the opportunities that have such a positive impact on future generations to come.

> *To give is a selfless action, and we can only give by sharing what we have.*

Giving is the greatest gift we possess. To give is a selfless action, and we can only give by sharing what we have. People can develop and practice their ability to give through acts of service, donating their time, compassion, love, money, comfort, advice, and anything or in any other way others need.

Volunteering encompasses the generosity of our time and energy without the expectation of compensation. To be present in an act for the sole purpose of contribution happened to align with my "soul" purpose, too.

Helping others in need has always been part of my life. My parents each escaped to Canada from communist Hungary as penniless refugees, my mother with her family when she was two, and my father when he was in his 30s. My parents met later in life, and everything they have achieved and built in this country came from vision and relentless ambition.

My father was given an incredible opportunity to work for a very powerful businessman who took a liking to him and saw his potential and coachability. With his mentoring, my father became a successful entrepreneur, and combined with my mother's unique skills and accomplishments, they made an impressively successful power couple.

Being raised in their house had many advantages. Growing up with an entrepreneur mindset gave me a totally different perspective on life and opportunities, lessons on endurance, and the desire for success. My mother taught me that entrepreneurs have a common misconception—the expectation of easy and quick success. The truth is, you must work hard, sacrificing personal and family time in order to achieve greatness.

As a family, we had many sacrifices, many obstacles, and many big breakthroughs. We were tried and tested, and somehow, we always found a way, just like water does. It might have to flow through, around, under, or in, but it will always fluidly adapt to its environment.

We are always impacted and affected by our environments. My childhood was wonderful, even difficult at times, but my parents, brother, and I always had each other. Knowing what I know now, I realize

73

those moments of struggles and great adversity truly forged the woman I have become. I've learned to heal my broken parts and find gratitude for the lessons, and I always find the light in the dark.

Our self-awareness always shifts and evolves. When we finally had money in our home, we finally had unlimited food, and I ate unlimited amounts. I never knew what "fat" was, and at home, I was cherished just the way I was. When I went to school, everyone bullied me as the fat kid. If you have ever been bullied physically or emotionally you know how cruel kids can be.

To make things worse, I became an emotional eater as the bullying continued. Though my weight caused pain and grief then, now I look at what happened as great blessings, because it became a protective barrier between me and almost anyone of the opposite sex. It also was easy to recognize who my true friends were— the ones who saw me on the inside, not just the outside.

In high school, I made a very dear friend, and from the moment I met Matthew Coatham I knew he was different. We developed a powerful bond, and he found beauty in all those parts of me that everyone else judged me for. He appreciated me for who I was, and how I was. He was also one of the funniest people I've met, and we share many interests, including our love of skiing and snowboarding.

Our group of friends was very close, and we competed with one another and pushed each other constantly, especially on the ski slope. I had never had friends like that before. I had the freedom of being myself and they accepted me for who I was. My looks didn't matter. They loved me for me.

Then the unimaginable happened and a great tragedy took my best friend, devastating everyone who knew him—family, friends, and the school. Losing him was the first big, painful lesson of my life, and still one of the most important. It taught me so much about appreciating the briefest moments in time with someone, and how deeply others can impact your vibration. I didn't realize until after his death how much I loved him; unfortunately, it was too late.

Somewhere I read that grief is love with nowhere to go. The hardest part after the loss of a loved one is learning how to live without them. It was a privilege to have shared all those laughs and smiles. His presence was a blessing. To have experienced him as energy, and to share so many beautiful adventures in our short time together. Memories are the truest gifts in life.

I began to live my life by one rule: *Love.*

The impact he made changed my perception of life, my reality, my understanding of how the world operates, and how quickly it is transformed when one piece of the puzzle is missing. I understood how powerful someone's energetic footprint can be and the ripple effect we have in our environments. I learned firsthand how we can resonate with people and how we can choose what impression we leave on them.

Of course, we can't control how others perceive us, but at least we can give them the roses they deserve while they can still smell them.

My second major moment was at a personal development event in Crete, Greece when I was asked a question that I was not prepared for. The trainer asked us, "Would you follow *you*?"

Without thinking, I blurted, "***No***." I was immediately devastated by my instant and honest dismissal of myself, and now I knew how far I was from being *that* leader, the leader that I would follow to the ends of the earth, the leader I was born to be.

Because I couldn't deny that I myself stood between me and my goals, I acknowledged I needed help and the right tools.

I had started my journey into personal development to see what I needed and now I realized I needed a lot of work. I'd reached that point all on my own. I'd spent lots of money traveling and learning from the best coaches, motivators, and inspirational speakers, but I knew that I was in desperate need of a complete mindset shift.

That mindset shift didn't begin until I began to acknowledge and understand my paradigms. I was trapped in old habits, my ego, and negative thoughts that no longer served me. I knew my mental process desperately needed an upgrade.

Let me paint you a picture. I felt like I was on my way to my castle, and suddenly, a huge gate blocked my path. I walked right up to the gate, grabbed its bars, and pressed my face into the space between them. I knew I didn't have the key, and there was no way I was going to be able to open this big gate without a key.

It took a while, but I finally discovered the key: *Learning to unlearn everything that no longer served me.* I needed to learn my lessons, then just release them as experiences. I discovered how to let go of situations, memories, traumas, and everything that was truly a burden to my mental health.

I began to nourish my mind with the right tools and resources, including the support of an excellent mindset coach, daily affirmations, audios, books, and visualizations. I began to understand the power of the mental world and how my outer world was shaping around me. Everything around me in my outer world reflected my current vibration and the frequency of my inner world. My environment, my circle of friends, my lifestyle, my accomplishments or lack thereof, were like mirrors and showed me where I was energetically.

As I learned more, I realized the gate had never been locked. I had seen the gate and its huge doors blocking me, and I had never tried to open it. I just assumed it was locked and accepted it as such.

George Addair gave us the most appropriate quote when he said, "Everything you've ever wanted is on the other side of fear." So true. Fear was my gate, a barrier of terror between me and all my dreams. The gate was just closed; it was never locked. The gate was a checkpoint that tested how badly I wanted to get to my castle.

This realization made me the magician in my own story, and the gate opened with a whimsical wave of a wand. With my wand I am in control, I am the author, the creator, and the champion of my own story.

I have always held that power, *as do you.* We each are our own creators, and the beauty of the creative process is that you get to co-create—co-create with yourself, each other, the universe, and all the infinite forms of creations that coexist and affect us in ways that are immeasurable.

Now, what vision did I create? My vision is to help billions of people and future generations find healing, love, success, and global acceptance. My YouTube Channel will bring blessings, positivity, and awareness to a wide audience around the world. It's focused on creating a safe community, and it shares my experiences in the hope that they will inspire others who may be going through similar situations. My mission is to reach others by sharing my vulnerability and personal struggles and impact them as powerfully as Johnny Wimbrey has impacted me.

78   A vision is what's created when individuals learn how to focus and set clear intentions to achieve this image in their minds through manifestation and determination. The power of the vision stems from the ability to visualize. Visualization is truly seeing, feeling, and being where you want to be, or doing what you want to do in your mind's eye. You must get passionate about your vision to the point that you elevate your emotional state and alter your physiology. This means raising your frequency to a higher vibration through motion, dance, or exercise.

See it, be it, feel it as if you are already there.

How do you visualize and create your vision? First, you need clarity on what you desire to achieve, receive, or become. A great example would be the measure of "clarity." Diamonds are great examples and their value is graded and measured by a scale of clarity. The clearer the diamond, the rarer, and more valuable it becomes, like a vision, which also requires an elite degree of clarity. How clear is your vision for how you see your life and your future? How does it feel being there? Who is with you celebrating your achievements?

Diamonds are created from immense amounts of pressure, so if you're feeling the pressure of life, please understand that you are simply experiencing the process required for you to become a diamond. The greater the pressure to achieve your vision, the more flawlessly rare you become during this chapter of your story.

I created a vision for that speech in Ireland, and I practiced the speech, over and over, for months. My visualization was so detailed that when I practiced the speech, it was as though my vision had become a reality. The real experience was very close to my visualization, though the lights were much hotter, and I delivered the message that God intended for me to give that day.

I was humbled when I realized how many people were impacted by my passion, a passion that helped ignite something within my listeners. I activated them to participate in volunteer programs, to help them expand and engage in their local communities, to have the vision of helping make a change in more lives.

Another event at which I had the honor of speaking was in Calmar, France, where I spoke in my third language, French. One of my favorite speakers used a guided meditation coaching technique like one Tony Robbins uses. She asked us to relax, close our eyes, and, with the aid of music, she told us to go back in time and visit our five-year-old self in a favorite memory.

At first, we were just observers, then we entered our memory and saw each other—five-year-old Edith and Edith as I am now. I looked at my young self; that little girl had dreams bigger than the universe. She was full of love, hope, innocence, and she was completely unprepared for the next 25 years of her life.

The present me has been through battles, wars, victories, and many defeats. There I stood, full of scars, broken parts, barely holding on, but still finding the strength to continue in life. I was full of a million emotions staring down at little Edith. I was in tears as she reminded me of the twinkle I'd had in my eyes, the confidence that entered the room before I did. She reminded me of the love that I have always had, my ability to love others, and to help lift them up from their darkest moments. She showed me I should still stand with those who can't carry themselves, embrace those who are confused, and help those who are giving up by giving them purpose.

Every single step in my life brought me here to this moment.

The little Edith has been within me the whole time. She has been begging me to not let the world destroy my dreams and put out my flames of desire and creativity. I cannot change the whole world alone, but I promise to change every single part of my world, everywhere I go.

I encourage you to spread your wings and break your chains. Don't focus on the life you have now, don't accept it as all you deserve—it's only one small aspect of the infinite possibilities available. Be the change! Be the difference! *You* have always been with *you* from the start. Love yourself, forgive yourself, and become your truest self, from now until forever.

The beautiful magic of life is the divine order in which everything falls into place even when it seems like it's falling apart. Balance will always be restored; it is the natural law.

If you lose something, it will be replaced with something better. To receive, we must first give. When you give with pure intentions, the law of reciprocity requires that in time you will receive something of equal or greater value.

Giving is the greatest gift of all.

Author's Notes

Known worldwide as Miss Edie, I am an entrepreneur, global volunteer, international speaker, humanitarian, mentor, philanthropist, network marketer, motivator, and spiritual consultant.

Together with World Ventures Foundation, I have donated resources and time to building schools in Guatemala and a medical clinic in Peru, upgrading orphanages in Czech Republic and Hungary, and performed many more acts of service worldwide. I also have provided thousands of nutritious meals to children and their families through the Ibüümerang Büüm Foundation.

I am a graduate of Carleton University in Ottawa, Canada, with a B.A. with Honors in Criminology and Justice Law, and also studied Forensic Sciences at the University of Toronto.

Contact information

Instagram: @missedie1
@missedietarot
YouTube: Miss Edie Tarot

Chapter 8

Consciousness, the Holy Grail of Mental Wealth

Jiri Urbanek

It is much better to have control over our lives and actions than to be a victim, letting ourselves be swept away by whatever circumstances happen to us. Adapting the practice of consciousness, a simple but powerful behavior makes everyone's life better.

Consciousness—being awake and aware of my surroundings—helped me to overcome the toughest times in my life. I know it can certainly help you, too.

Even though we don't like to admit it, our subconscious minds are programmed by what affects us from outside. During any crisis (and it doesn't matter if it's a personal one or a worldwide pandemic), we keep hearing a drumbeat of fear and disaster: Everything is going wrong, nothing is going right. Our minds follow those drums right down the path of despair, making the situation even worse than it is.

When that happens, it is the right time to increase consciousness using common sense: *Challenge the status quo.* Ask questions and start to think rationally. Avoid being manipulated by emotions, wrong models, prejudice, and manipulations, both your own and those created by others.

> *Consciousness, gratefulness, hope, and optimism are the hallmarks of those who are open to change, welcome responsibility, and use all possibilities that they actively discover.*

84

Realize the power of emotion and learn to not succumb to it; instead, use it for your own benefit. That is what it's all about.

I'll give you an example. When I was diagnosed with multiple sclerosis in 2009, an incurable neurological disease that may lead to full disability, I fell into a very deep depression. I was paralyzed by fear. Rhetorical, stupid questions popped up in my mind every day: *Why me? What caused it?* I searched for information about the disease on the internet, called friends who were doctors, and read everything I could.

Despite my own medical education and knowledge, I did not find any information anywhere that gave me reason to hope. I was only able to create negative scripts in my mind, thinking about the day when I would stop walking and spend the rest of my life lying on my bed. As my life became more and more desperate, I envisioned every possible bad outcome from the disease. Though I received the best treatment, I did not expect any improvement because I was ready to be disabled in the future.

That is the power of negative thinking.

Even worse, I started to transfer my negativity to others. I was mean to people around me, even my children. I saw myself as a victim without control over my life, and what's even sadder, I started to like it. If there was something, I did not want to do, or I screwed up, I always had an excuse: "What do you want from me? I am seriously ill."

One day I realized I could not live my life that way. I had already lost my independence and freedom to my fear and illness, and even my ability to make good decisions was fast being eroded. Living like that was devastating me and the people around me, those whom I loved the most. I started to increase my consciousness and think rationally. I evaluated my condition objectively, from the outside, as I would for someone else. Without fear or negativity—without emotions.

I began to see the positive aspects. I became grateful that I could still walk and do almost everything I did before, just with minor limitations. I changed my mindset from victim to creator, bit by bit.

As I set a goal to live a full, high-quality life, I made a plan. Positivity, gratefulness, and hope were the first steps, then I began to change my bad habits and eliminate the aggravators of my disease. I accepted the fact that my disease was a consequence of my earlier bad decisions. This was not about being sorry about what happened, but about conscious analysis of causes. Health is closely connected with the mental setup and attitude to life. And I consciously helped my doctors by maintaining an active, optimistic attitude and the desire to regain my lost health.

This was not easy, but good things don't come the easy way. It took me three years of my life to make these changes. Consciousness helped me to gain my life back. Today, I live my life at 100% of my health and capacity. I'm happy, satisfied, and I can do anything without limitations.

That episode of my life clearly showed me we attract whatever we feel and believe. If you are focused on bad things, bad things happen. Such is the power of our consciousness, whether spoken or thought. It is up to us whether it unfolds in a good or a bad direction.

Believe it or not, you can influence the way a situation unfolds with your positive mindset.

But it is tricky. Our subconscious always tries to pull us back, back to our "easy" life, actions, and habits—even if they are bad for us. If you let your subconscious win, you will never succeed.

Our habits, actions, and behavioral traditions are very resistant to change. Once you aren't one of the sheep in a herd any longer, people start to think that something is wrong with you. They don't accept your freedom to choose your way. They try to pull you back, blaming you, even attacking you, simply because they want you to be like them. Often, they use emotional pressure.

A surprising number of people live their lives within the artificial boundaries they've defined for themselves. How many times did you want something but held back? I am sure you found some rational explanation why it was impossible—*It's too difficult . . . it would be selfish*—or the immortal phrase *I'll do it later.*

When you're on your deathbed, all those self-imposed restrictions will cause you to say *I did not live the life I wanted.* Why? It's because we erect barriers to keep us from taking advantage of the possibilities.

When you ask people why they remain in conditions that suck, you'll hear, *It cannot be changed; I have had this all my life; I cannot do it; or What would people say.* What nonsense! It's just their indolence and a false sense of security. What they're really saying is, *It sucks but I am in control.* The stereotypes we create simplify the processing of information and automate mental processes. We're not aware because stereotypical reactions are automatic and subconscious.

Consciousness opens your eyes to see a different world. It is really hard to resist your subconscious, but you can choose to reject an emotionally conditioned request or extortion. You have the right to make your own choices at any given moment. The other party's reaction to the decision is *their* choice. Do they choose to be sad, offended, irritated, silent, or to rejoice and be happy? Their reaction is *not* your business, not ever! *We are only responsible for our own feelings! Period, full stop.*

Our emotions do shake us up from time to time despite ourselves, and then we ask *what did we do wrong? How can we make it right again?* This is a higher level of consciousness.

Our conscious and subconscious selves are hardwired inside our brains. The part of our brains called neocortex is responsible for rational decisions, analytical behavior, and speech. The more primitive part of the brain, the limbic, is responsible for emotions such as trust, loyalty, behavior, decisions, and reinforcing behavior. The limbic does not control speech, so it can't speak up rationally and join the conversation with the neocortex.

If we manage to communicate with the limbic system using emotional communication, we hit the decision-making spot directly. That is why we prefer to accept emotional messages rather than using analytical thinking, and that's what hurts us in critical situations.

It's very important to control our thinking. How many times a day do you catch yourself thinking of something other than you intended to? Too often it's negative thoughts, re-evaluating something that happened in the past that affected our performance poorly. Even though we know that we can't change or control the past, our minds easily get trapped into thinking about our mistakes and failures.

Don't we agree in theory that if we cannot control or change something, we should never let it distract us? We can clearly see this distraction affecting athletes in particular. Rather than concentrating on their performance, they have all sorts of negative thoughts running through their mind, *especially* the times they performed badly in the past—and so their current performance is doomed.

It's daily work to improve and strengthen our consciousness. One of the most important actions we can take is to make an appointment with ourselves. This quiet time with ourselves is insightful, helping us to sort out our thoughts and make sure we're going in the right direction. We get strength to fulfill our resolutions and to define other, better resolutions and goals. We should find room for improvement and progress.

It's not that complicated. Reach for an interesting book, meditate, calm down, and think of yourself. The best way for me is to relax and think is while cruising in my 1968 Buick.

Perhaps you're afraid of what problems you'll find when you are alone with yourself, in peace and quiet? Don't worry, the realization that something is amiss is the beginning of the conversion to becoming a creator. *Before any progress, there must be acknowledgment there's dissatisfaction with the current state of affairs.*

89

I perform this exercise often and it always leads me to new decisions. It's about finding a good balance between emotions and rational thinking.

We have to survive in our environment—in our community, family, school, work—so we can't do whatever we want. Well, we *can*, but we then have to accept the consequences. In any case, we can set acceptable boundaries and create our unique vision of freedom and success. It is in our hands.

My plan for change always starts with defining *why* I want to make this change. With more age and experience, my vision of my life's purpose is shifting away from just my own paycheck and well-being to helping others and seeing the wider picture. Yes, money is important, yet consciousness helps us develop a desire for fulfillment, doing something to help people around us, something of real value.

This happened to me a few years ago. I was a successful manager in a pharmaceutical company, thinking I was living the white-collar, upper-middle-class life. Instead, I was actually living in a golden cage. For many years, I believed the pharma industry helps people to get better treatment, so I convinced myself I was really helping people. As I became more involved in the inner workings of the business, I learned it doesn't have much to do with helping people. Pharma is purely a money-making business, fighting for market share and profit while being wrapped in a façade of helping people.

I trained people on how to present pharmaceutical products, how to communicate, even how to balance on the fine edge between promotion and manipulation. I developed a method called *Emotional Selling.* The positive effect on sales and profit was enormous in every European country where I implemented it. But there was a little problem: Emotional Selling does not follow pharma industry myths, rigid rules, and old habits. It's more about finding self-confidence and people's positive mindset. It is more about finding a common need and solution than about a simple victory over someone. In sum, it's about how to avoid being manipulated.

This was my first step in the direction of helping others. I realized "normal" people need such training more than salespeople and managers. So, I created emotional selling for "normal people," and described the process in a book I wrote with a provocative title: *I Take No Sh*t.* (By the way, it's only available in Czech; the English version is still in the works.)

I found my *why*—my purpose in life—and it's to help others. That is good, but how do I manage it? On one side, I found my passion; on the other hand, I had bills to pay.

So, like most people in similar situations, I made the wrong decision. I kept my job and my financial stability, and I postponed escaping my golden cage.

I know now that if there is something in your life that you don't like, you must change it quickly. Consciously find the time to look for opportunities and do not be afraid of changes. Expect some effort, hard work, and discomfort, even criticism, and displeasure from others. If, however, your goal is motivated by your heart and desire and based on common sense, you will succeed—*and you will be happy.*

I stayed in my golden cage and lived my unsatisfactory life until 2019. That was the toughest year of my life. Really.

On January 2, 2019, my father suddenly died. On the same day, a postman brought me a foreclosure notice for our house, a result of the debts my father left, and I was given two weeks to put together $9,000 to avoid default. In March, I was fired from my job with the pharma company. Later that year, my mother attempted suicide and ended up in a psychiatric hospital for four months, and I traveled 200 miles twice a week to visit her. In May, my partner Lucie went on a six-month sick leave, which was followed by her losing her pharma industry job, too.

A tough year, right? Yet I survived all this because I was able to consciously manage every problem, solving one issue after another, setting clear goals and solutions. That does not mean that the crises didn't affect my emotions; emotions are always there. Anger, sadness, excitement, desperation . . . everything you can imagine. It is really easy to succumb to the negative and blame the world, God, or whomever, and sit in a corner and cry, but those are the actions of a victim.

Do not blame the world around you for your miserable life, do not pity yourself, and do not complain. That's how victims behave. A creator, on the other hand, decides what will happen.

92

Living through sad moments does not prevent us from having an optimistic view of life; just live through the situation and put it aside. Even a bad situation brings something good. It was meant to teach us something, but we learn and then don't need it anymore. Realization and learning are positive things. *Be positive.*

Here are the lessons I learned:

Consciousness, gratefulness, hope, and optimism are the hallmarks of those who are open to change, welcome responsibility, and use all possibilities that they actively discover. Let us be grateful for what we have even though we ask for more. Gratitude and appreciation are signs of maturity. Consciousness helps you manage all the situations life brings. Consciousness helps you find solutions and make plans, and it keeps you focused on problem-solving.

Everything was turned upside—in a very positive way—in 2019. The drastic changes and the problems I solved strengthened my trust in consciousness and its importance. It also sorted the people around me. It really showed who I can rely on to stand by my side during the hard times, my real friends. I am grateful for these people around me, especially my partner, Lucie. She helped me so, so much.

When my life changed in 2019, I was 47 years old. Now I fully enjoy my freelance existence. I have a chance to really help people, and not only in my private life. I finished my MBA and found a passion for network marketing. I love it. I love the equity of the MLM system, love the real cooperation, and the ability to help others to succeed.

Be aware, determination of success is only in our heads. Believe it or not, we can *attract* success by conscious positive thinking, confidence, and a positive mindset. In other words, everyone has the capacity to achieve whatever they want.

How do we do it? Emotions are manageable, and I have already demonstrated that by controlling them we increase our potential for success. Our limits are only in our minds. Once we admit this, we can start pushing the limits. *Consciously!*

Author's Notes

My training as a veterinarian led me to work as a teacher and researcher at the University of Veterinary and Pharmaceutical Sciences in Brno, Czech Republic. Later, I entered the pharmaceutical industry, working in senior managerial positions with an international agenda. I spent almost twenty years in the pharma industry; my focus was

94

on business planning, business development, business ethics and compliance, communication, sales, marketing, people management, and development.

I developed a unique communication/selling concept called Emotional Selling, which helps people be more effective in communication and in finding win/win solutions. Using this concept, I wrote *I Take No Sh*t*, a book that transferred these emotional selling principles to private-life situations. Though it's currently available only in Czech, it's in the process of being published in English.

In 2019, I made the biggest change in my entire life and permanently left the golden cage of corporate business to run my own business. Now through consulting, business training, and coaching, I spend my time trying to help people to have a better life.

My degrees include a doctorate in veterinary medicine (DVM), and a master's degree in business administration (MBA). I've been a baseball youth coach for ten years.

I cherish my sons Tomas and Lukas (15 and 11), and my two-year-old daughter, Agata. My fiancée and business partner, Lucie, and I live in Valasske Mezirici in the Czech Republic. I'm grateful to Lucie for her inspiration and support, without which I would never have had the courage to change my life.

Contact Information:

Email: jura.urbos@gmail.com   95
Facebook: Jiri Urbanek, EmocniprodejCZ
LinkedIn: www.linkedin.com/in/drjiriurbanek
Instagram: @EmocniprodejCZ
Twitter: @EmocniprodejCZ

96

Chapter 9

You're Gonna Make It After All

Toni L. Pennington

I'm gonna write through it, cry through it,
live through it, love through it,
pray through it,
be blue through it,
but I'm going to get through it.

Research and experience tell me mental health directly correlates with mental wealth. The *Oxford English Dictionary* (OED) defines health as, "Soundness of body; that condition in which its functions are duly and efficiently discharged." The OED defines wealth as, "The condition of being happy and prosperous; well-being." Combined, the two suggest that being mentally and emotionally healthy, and making sure you are in a good place with both, will produce a wealth of body, mind, soul, and spirit.

I'm not a psychologist, but it sure makes sense to me. That good place—that sweet spot—sounds like the place we'd all like to be.

We're going through a dark time in our history, and it makes that sweet spot more difficult to visualize and attain. It's important that we try, however, for the work we do right now will make us better, healthier, and stronger for an uncertain future.

Most of us don't realize the depth of our mental wealth until we face astounding situations.

So far, 2020 has been an extremely difficult year for every human being on earth. At the time of this writing, we are all learning what it means to show love from an acceptable social distance, what it means to cook every meal at home, and, for many of us, what it means to reconnect with our families. The coronavirus pandemic has taught us how to live alone together (no, that is not an oxymoron). It has also given us an opportunity to spend time with ourselves, our thoughts, and our deepest feelings. We have the rare opportunity to be silent and reflective.

I had no idea this would be one of the most painful times in my life.

I have written about surviving traumatic situations before, but never while I was in the midst of one. As I write this chapter, I have just suffered a devastating loss. The unimaginable happened—the love of my life died suddenly.

In my previous writings, I didn't share his name because people aren't always glad for you when you're happy. They don't always root for you, unfortunately. We were very private about our relationship, and that allowed us to nurture it and give it what it needed without prying eyes or opinions. Within our bubble, we added to each other's lives. The decision to maintain our privacy allowed our collective mental wealth to grow and strengthen. We healed and made each other better; those details are for a different story. One day, perhaps.

My love was the world-renowned, Grammy-award-winning drummer and percussionist Jeff "LO" Davis. He was known as the Godfather of Gospel Drumming. In his nearly four-decade career, he appeared on over 300 albums and worked in almost every musical genre. Jeff played with everyone from Richard Smallwood to Sting to Stevie Wonder.

While he wasn't a household name, among his peers, colleagues, and those he tutored and mentored, Jeff was a highly respected, polished, professional musician with his own distinct sound. He was a teacher and lover of music and an even greater lover of God and the gospel of Jesus Christ. He was a good man who always had ministry on his mind, whether it was feeding the homeless, making their lives better, or teaching young musicians how they should behave and carry themselves in church as well as in the music industry.

On many occasions, I watched musicians of every age hang onto Jeff's every word and motion as he conducted clinics. They knew he had seen it all. Jeff generously shared his mental wealth, pouring out everything he had, praying that what he offered would enhance the lives of those around him. To my amazement, Jeff didn't realize how beloved and unique he was. On the drive home, he would be shocked as I shared what I witnessed: Everyone in the room had been on the edge of their seats, taking in his every word. His humility was overwhelming. We were only granted six short years together, but they were rich years. I am brokenhearted but still grateful.

The desire to share knowledge is something we had in common. As a tutor, I take great pleasure in giving what I have if it helps the student reach their goal. I understand why sharing is called "the gift of giving." There is a profound feeling of fulfillment when you give someone else what they need. When you give freely, you change lives. Sometimes you will never know who you've reached; people may appear years later and let you know how a small thing you did or said changed their life. If that's not powerful, I don't know what is!

My brother says there is a nugget of selfishness in sharing: While you accomplish a good deed, you in turn feel good about yourself. I agree, but it's more complex than just stroking your ego. Externally, it appears that you are giving something; doing a good deed, but internally you experience a change. That change fortifies you. It enhances your sense of kindness, caring, and empathy. That practice helps stock your mental wealth treasure chest. It helps free you from the guilt of selfishness and puts what is good in your life into perspective. You probably know the saying,

"I cried when I had no shoes, then I met a man with no feet"

—**Mahatma Gandhi**

Being able to share what you've learned is the ultimate mental wealth. When you are a giving person, rich in kindness and love, it is my experience that the same comes back to you exponentially.

There is a caveat: You should always give from your heart, never with the expectancy of a reward. Give graciously with an unexpectant heart and allow the blessings to fall upon you when it's time. That time will most likely be when you need something the most.

You may be asking, what was the point of telling you of my loss? Well, what I needed for my mental wealth changed. When Jeff died, I was finishing a graduate school class, in the midst of trying to push through my final project, and I was struggling. Ironically, I was working on two papers, one entitled "What Does Loss Feel Like", and the other, "I Don't Remember Crying." Talk about foreshadowing.

Universities don't have generous bereavement policies for their students, so I was forced to focus and push through my grief as I researched and wrote my papers. I knew how proud Jeff was of my work, and that was instrumental in my getting the job done. He always told me he admired me and I inspired him every day with my work ethic as it related to my studies and my students. I didn't realize he was silently watching me, and Jeff didn't know his words replenished me; they meant so much because I admired and respected him. Yes, we had a low-key, mutual admiration society. I kept his words, gestures, and memories stored in my mental health chest, where they sustained me and my mental wealth as I grieved.

That leads me to the concept of knowing what you need. As a writer, you can become detached from the subject matter, paying closer attention to the process, making sure your writing makes sense, flows well, and is understandable. You just look at the words objectively. I became so engrossed in the work I didn't notice how personal the stories were and where they were headed.

Each story unwrapped a time of profound crisis in my life, a calamity during which I had to find mental wealth, a way to survive. The loss of my mother at a very young age and my own devastating, life-changing health issues were the basis of the stories. I had no intention of going so deeply into past pain and healing, but it was clear I needed this catharsis because once again my life changed. This new tragedy was even more surreal, and all of this was happening as the whole world shifted course and was learning to navigate a plague.

To maintain my mental wealth and health, I deliberately faced my own feelings.

Logically, I knew it would do me no good to try to act like everything was the same because it wasn't. I had to accept my life had changed and I had to change with it.

I made a decision to feed my mind with positive things, happy memories, and pleasant thoughts. I had a lot to draw from in the midst of my sadness, and it was stored in my mental wealth treasure chest. I used the necessary amounts to get through the end of that class. I used a little more to get through the next one. Intuitively, I realized I needed to always keep something on reserve.

Don't get me wrong. I wasn't skipping around the house acting like everything was great. I cried when I needed to cry. I still do. I stopped when I needed to stop, and I felt the heartache when something as simple as someone clapping the same way he did would remind me that I could only hear him in my dreams. There was no getting around that. But exercising my right (and filling my need) to feel a full range of emotions contributed to my mental wealth, my stockpile of wealth builders, which I am happy to share.

Know what you need. This can be a little tricky because initially, you may not know what that is. Sometimes we don't realize what works for us until a situation is forced upon us. For example, you may need to get out and get some fresh air. You've been perfectly happy inside, but after you go outdoors, let a breeze brush your face or hear the birds sing, you may realize how restorative a change of scenery can be.

Another example is good old-fashioned laughter. That one really works for me. When I was diagnosed with HIV, I was afraid that I would never laugh again. On my way home from that appointment, I saw something really funny and burst into a long, loud crack-up in my

103

car. I was grateful because I felt as though God, at that moment, heard my plea for some sense of normalcy, and He answered immediately. It felt like a miracle. These things contribute to your mental wealth and well-being.

Know when you need to talk. Generally, we can feel when we need to speak to someone. We might need a therapist or just a sympathetic ear, someone who knows you and is aware of what you are going through. Perhaps it might be someone who doesn't know what's happening with you, but you trust and rely on their wisdom and sensitivity. Use your judgment.

Know when you need silence. When word was getting out that my love had died, I was sitting at home alone. My brother and several of my sister-friends immediately wanted to come to my aid. "We won't say anything if you don't want, we'll just be there." The cities and states were just beginning to lock down so my sister couldn't get to me.

Thank God for love. I was so appreciative of their offers, but my heartache was so big that there was no room in my home for anyone or anything but me and my pain. I knew that another human being in my space would just annoy me, even if they didn't say a word. I truly needed to be alone and mourn in silence. I didn't have the capacity to worry about anyone else's feelings if I burst into tears if I wanted to roll around on the floor and scream, if I wanted to cut off all my hair (I wasn't going quite that far), but I was sure I needed to be by myself.

Know when you need space and when you need company. Two days into my grief, I asked my brother if he would come over. He did. When he was ready to leave, I didn't want him to go. I had switched from wanting to be alone to needing the comfort of his presence. I realized each situation gave me strength and security because the timing had been right.

When I was alone, I was wrapped in Jeff's love, and there was no room for anyone else in my space. That would have been an intrusion. That time was only meant for Jeff and me. When my brother came, he knew I was trying to be strong. When he hugged me, I turned into a bag of water and let out the tears I didn't know I had been holding. Then we sat silently until I cried again. I did not know what I needed. Thank God others did.

What happens when you're not sure what you need? What works for me is being still and giving my spirit the chance to tell me. It's finding ways to feed my mind and my heart.

Building mental wealth isn't much different than accumulating financial wealth. You've got to figure out what it will take for you to survive (or thrive) in much the same way you calculate the income you need to live comfortably. To do this right, you must take some private time and sit, perhaps meditate, and ask yourself the hard questions. No one else will listen in, so you can tell yourself the pure, unadulterated truth. Then write it down and hide it in a safe place where your thoughts cannot be compromised.

Most of us don't realize the depth of our mental wealth until we face astounding situations. When we look back, we're amazed at the way we handled them. I challenge you to look over your life and find at least one experience where you didn't think you would make it but you did.

That is your triumph—your treasure chest of mental wealth.

Author's Notes

Though I've been a singer since my childhood, my creative energy is now focused on my writing. I've been published many times in *PATHS,* a literary publication of New Jersey City University. In 2018, I co-authored *Break Through featuring Toni L. Pennington* with Les Brown and several international authors. More recently, I co-authored *P.U.S.H.: Persist Until Success Happens,* with Matt Morris, Johnny Wimbrey, Sashin Govender, and other well-known authors. My books are found on my own website, listed below, and on Amazon.

I hold a Bachelor of Arts degree in English from New Jersey City University, where I work as an academic success coach and tutor mentor, and I'm completing a Master of Arts degree at Southern New Hampshire University. I was born in Brooklyn, New York, and now live in Jersey City, New Jersey.

Contact Information

Email: joyforeverenterprises@gmail.com
Website: joyforeverenterprises.com
Instagram: @Joyforever1love

Chapter 10

State of Mind Transforms 'Underdog' into 'Overdog'*

Donnie Lewis

"May I read a chapter from my book, *I Know Why the Caged Bird Sings?*"

I didn't realize it at the time, but this one question would permanently change my views of self-development, positive thinking, and motivational awareness. I've known and used these concepts since I was young, but I'd rarely opened a book. At that moment, I was being introduced to a new genre and a new chapter in my life.

It was March 26, 1998, in Winston-Salem, North Carolina. I was Trisha Yearwood's tour manager, and we were on tour with Garth Brooks. The day before the

---

*__Overdog:__ Dominant, in command, or with significant advantage.

Winston-Salem show, Maya Angelou's agent called: Dr. Angelou wanted to invite Trisha, her assistant, and me to her home for lunch the next day before the evening show. We were thrilled to accept the invitation.

The three of us arrived at her house and waited in the foyer. When she gracefully walked down the steps to greet us, I was already in awe—she almost seemed like royalty. We visited, strolled through her sculpture garden, and then she prepared a lunch of pork chops.

An uphill battle always fired me up, and then then someone told me I couldn't do something I wanted to do, they really poured fuel on the fire

After lunch, she asked that life-changing question about reading a chapter from her famed book, and our answer was a unanimous *yes!*. She began reading, and we were mesmerized by every word. We heard the chapter come to life from the author's own voice.

I thought to myself, *who gets to experience this?* That night I realized how exceptional that opportunity actually had been when a local journalist covering the show told us that a lunch or dinner with Dr. Angelou was a rare and coveted invitation in Winston-Salem.

The day after our visit, I did some research and discovered that early in her career Angelou was called "The Voice of the Underdog." It helped me understand why I related to her so well because I've owned the unenviable title of underdog all too often in my life.

Angelou had a rare trait of relating to people from all walks of life and backgrounds. Early in her life, an anxiety disorder from childhood traumas led to her not speaking for five years; she's said her listening and observing skills expanded during those years. She credits those characteristics for helping her become more successful in her career, taking a negative and turning it into a positive, being an underdog who became an overdog. She became an award-winning author, poet, and screenwriter.

The words she read to us that fateful day had changed me, and I became a voracious reader, especially motivational books. Her reading was an eye-opening experience for me that I will never forget because I witnessed firsthand someone truly gifted with *the power of mental wealth.*

And it's not as though I had been impressed by meeting a celebrity; I've met hundreds during my career as a tour manager, including several presidents, many professional athletes, and entertainers.

You may not know what being a tour manager entails. Most people don't, and when I'm interviewed, usually the first question is, "What exactly *is* a tour manager?" My standard tongue-in-cheek answer is, "An executive babysitter!"

But, in all seriousness, tour managers wear many hats: travel, logistics, bus and plane leasing, tour accounting, and responsibility for overseeing the entire tour. I have to say, I'm one of the most fortunate tour managers to have ever stepped onto a tour bus or jet. I would never have dreamed I'd work alongside music icons Tammy Wynette, Trisha Yearwood, and Peter Frampton for more than 25 years. I often say that my reality has put my dreams to shame.

When I was a boy growing up in Gratis, Ohio, a small rural town with a population of about 650, it was assumed I would work a blue-collar type job, just as my family has been doing for generations. We didn't give it much thought, and it was just a given that my future was to be a factory worker.

When I was eighteen, my father told me that an application was waiting at the paper mill where he had worked for years. I remember saying, "Thanks, but I'm going to be a professional drummer." To my dad, my plans were as farfetched as if I'd said I was flying to Mars. To him playing drums had no place in adult reality; it was a weekend hobby, not a career.

My mother always knew I would be a drummer. I had been drumming on her kitchen pots and pans since I was a toddler, and I soon graduated to a collection of toy drums. At a teacher/parent conference, my third-grade teacher told her that I was driving the other students crazy, always drumming on my desk with my pencils. My mother believed in me, and somehow she managed to wear down the rest of the family's resistance. I am forever grateful to her.

I was a rapturous seven-year-old when I unwrapped a set of drums on Christmas morning, purchased by my mom from a small town retailer, Western Auto for a whopping $19.95. This set of drums was real enough to set up at our little country church and play in services every Thursday and Sunday. I played for that small congregation for years, and that was a valuable learning experience, but I knew I was ready to perform to a different audience. I wanted to be in a band—a real band.

In the summer before eighth grade, the band instructor visited our house to discuss her plans for me in the marching band. She told my parents I wasn't good enough yet to play the snare drum and recommended I play cymbals instead.

I refused. Playing cymbals was *not* a viable substitute for playing drums, it was *not* going to happen; my mind was set on being a *drummer*. This was the first time I was an underdog. I *would* find a way, whatever it took, to play drums in public! I passed on the cymbals.

Very soon I heard that a local gospel band was hiring a drummer. I auditioned—and I landed the job! While my friends were sweating, spending long hours on the football field practicing, I traveled regionally for concerts with my band—*and* I was getting paid to do it.

This became the story of my life. From an early age, I usually started as the underdog. An uphill battle always fired me up, and then when someone told me I couldn't do something I wanted to do, they really poured fuel on the fire. More often than not, I'd get what I wanted. I'd become the overdog.

"Overdog" isn't a common expression, but I hope it starts to become one. Underdogs do *not* need to remain trapped in their lowly status; once they begin to win, their status changes to dominant, they're in control, and they become the overdogs.

I have a good overdog example for you. In 1977, before my junior year of high school, I applied to a technical school now known as Miami Valley Career Technology Center, where I wanted to complete my junior and senior years. I was considering a career working with animals, possibly as a zoologist or veterinarian.

Mr. Frisby, my high school guidance counselor, was a kind man. When he learned I had applied, he called me into his office to soften the inevitable blow. "Donnie," he told me, "it's unlikely you will get accepted because it's one of the more popular courses at that school. Only 25 students will be accepted from nearly two hundred that applied, so don't expect to be chosen."

Realizing I was once again the underdog, I drove forty-five minutes to that school and convinced the course advisor to meet me during his lunch break. I looked at him and said confidently, "Mr. Johnson, if you don't choose me, it will be a big mistake. I will outwork the other students and you won't regret selecting me."

Mr. Johnson and I were together in October 2016, and we looked back at that moment and chuckled. Not only did I convince him to select me for the course, in 2016 I became the 39th student in the school's forty-nine-year history to be inducted into the school's Hall of Fame. Through the years, more than 88,200 students have walked the halls of that school, yet the short, scrawny, underdog kid has his Hall of Fame plaque on the wall.

In the press interviews at the Hall of Fame ceremony, I forgot to thank my guidance counselor, Mr. Frisby; I will do it here. While I know he was trying to protect me from probable disappointment, at the time I didn't see it that way. I'm thankful that he poured fuel on the fire without even realizing it.

After graduating from tech school, I was at a crossroad. Should I choose a career in animal husbandry or a music career? At that moment, I received an unexpected call from The Mid-South Boys, a band located in Sheridan, Arkansas. I only had regional experience as a drummer, but this underdog was determined. I got the job and that turned into an eight-year career. Against many odds, we were offered a record deal with a major label, moved to Nashville, Tennessee, and the record company eventually suggested a name change to simply MidSouth,

The years spent touring with that band were some of the best times of my life.

After my drumming career came to an end, I knew I wanted to remain in the music industry. A couple of friends were tour managers; I was intrigued and asked enough questions to decide tour management would be my new career. I had a pretty good skillset in logistics and organization, but with no experience, it seemed to be a longshot. As I prepared a new résumé, I knew I was an underdog again.

After several months of knocking on doors, sending résumés, and getting rejected in interviews, I got a call from a friend who was Tammy Wynette's tour manager. He was planning to move on, and he said I would be a great fit to replace him as tour manager. Could this be it? It was a dream job with a country music legend. Though I learned six other candidates were in the running for the position, my friend said it'd be a good experience to interview in any case.

I had the interview, and it went well. As I was walking out the door, Ricky Skaggs' office manager called and asked if I could interview later that same afternoon. I LOVED his music! Two major interviews in one day.

I had no doubt I was going to be hired for one of those two tour manager positions . . . period.

By day's end, I was an overdog! I had a big decision to make.

The Wynette tour became my choice, based solely on the fact that Tammy was going on a European tour and I had never been out of the United States.

I have countless other underdog stories; maybe you have your own. Possibly you are at a crossroads in life, feeling discouraged because things aren't going your way, you feel stuck, and you can't seem to get out of a mental rut? It's time to change your attitude, and it all starts with personal development.

Consider this, if you don't make financial deposits, you will not develop *financial wealth*! And, as importantly, if you don't make mental deposits you won't develop *mental wealth*! I want to help you make good sound mental wealth investments.

Recommendations for personal development

Often business students, musicians, and young entrepreneurs ask me, *What should I read? What will help me get to the next level? How do I get noticed?* And, of course, *How do I get an interview*? My answer is always the same: ***It starts with personal development, which leads to mental wealth***. In an interview or a mentoring session, I can usually identify those who have worked with personal development materials.

I have a huge library written by some of the best personal development and motivational authors in the world. Here are a few recommendations, some that have helped in my music and entrepreneurial career.

Books

- *Music, Money, and Success*, by Jeffrey Brabec and Todd Brabec
- *Life Is a Contact Sport*, by Ken Kragen, an entertainer/artist manager
- *The Slight Edge*, by Jeff Olson
- *Living Your Life in Peak Performance*, by Scott Speight
- *From the Hood to Doing Good*, by Johnny Wimbrey

Speakers and trainers

- *Marc Accetta*, one of the best trainers I've ever experienced. He trains in a unique way, using characters and skits on stage to convey his message to his audiences.
- *Matt Morris*, The Unemployed Millionaire. I get fired up every time I hear him speak.
- *Bethany Webster*, a friend and great speaker. Her speaking tends to focus on posturing up. She has been very influential in my life.

I'm confident that the great authors in this book will touch many lives and help underdogs to become overdogs. I can't wait to hear *your* story!

Afterword

While I was working on *The Power of Mental Wealth*, disaster struck in my hometown of Mt. Juliet, Tennessee. EF3 and EF4 tornadoes ripped through four counties and traveled more than sixty miles, destroying schools, businesses, and homes. I was in Washington, D.C., when the call came at 2 a.m., and I was warned I wouldn't recognize parts of my community when I returned home. Indeed, that was the case. Upon my return three days later, I drove to an area where nearly every house was flattened and I walked the streets to see if there was any way I could help. When I walked up to a house with only one room still standing, I met a young lady in the driveway, and asked, "Is there anything I can do to help?"

She said quietly, "Just pray for my neighbors."

I agreed to do that, then I asked, "Was your family able to salvage anything?"

"Our entire family's lives! That's all that matters. We have each other, we will come out stronger."

I'd ventured out that day to see if I could be of some small blessing. It turned out *I* was the one that received the blessing. Her words moved me, and I will never forget her concern for others, her unshakable faith, and her calmness in the middle of heartbreaking devastation. It was evident she embodied the power of mental wealth.

After this book is published and she and her family rebuild, I look forward to visiting her family's new home. I will stroll down Barrett Street once again, hand her the first copy of *The Power of Mental Wealth*, and let her know how powerfully she affected me on the day we first met.

Author's Notes

My life has always been filled with music, and I began touring regionally with professional bands while still in junior high school. For eight years, I was the touring drummer with the band MidSouth as they won several major industry awards and recorded many top-charting songs. I'm still a member of the Country Music Association.

I've been a Nashville-based tour manager for the majority of my working life, working for Tammy Wynette, Trisha Yearwood, and Peter Frampton, and organizing successful tours in all 50 states and 28 countries. I've also worked with artists at all major award shows including the Grammys, Oscars, and the Academy of Country Music Awards.

As a specialist at travel, scheduling, and logistics, I've been entrusted with those duties for many sports and entertainment celebrities. I've been honored to be a keynote speaker at universities, business events, and music trade shows across the country, and have been invited to the White House four times. I've become an outspoken advocate of early detection as a cancer survivor.

I've led teams in the direct sales arena with members in all 50 states, Asia, and Europe, helping underdogs become overdogs.

I was born in Southern Ohio, and currently live in Mt. Juliet, Tennessee.

Contact information

Email: tourmgr7@aol.com
Facebook: Donnie Lewis
Twitter: @donnielewis
Instagram: @donnielewistourmgr

Chapter 11

Be Invincible!

Therease L. Thompson

Kids were rushing by, running in circles on the school playground, trying to generate the slightest breeze, laughing and excited about recess on a hot, humid Mississippi day. As usual, I was alone, hanging upside down by my legs on the monkey bars. An unfamiliar sense of peace overwhelmed me, and in a moment of lucidity, I relaxed my legs. The fall was effortless as if at that moment, gravity was my only friend. I was five years old. That was the first time I attempted suicide.

I awoke in the hospital, disoriented and disappointed that I'd failed. When bombarded with questions, instead of answering truthfully, I retreated further into my cocoon of fake smiles and solitude. I would keep my secret for many years—until this moment.

My torment began a couple of years earlier when I was three and my uncle Michael picked me up from my first day of preschool, and it continued with my stepfather Fred, uncle Kerry, and cousin Joe until I was almost 14. I felt betrayed by the people who were supposed to protect me —by my family, by my mother . . . by God. I didn't know the words for what

> *Whatever we choose to focus on is what will grow, whether it's in our thoughts, our souls, our lives, or our futures.*

was happening to me, and only later learned them: abuse, rape, incest, and molestation.

As the youngest of my mother's daughters, I often wondered what made me such a target for sexual abuse. Like most children, I blamed it on my differences. In my African-American Louisiana family, my light skin made me stand out like a bright yellow dandelion in a perfectly manicured lawn—beautiful, but still unwanted. I still associate attention with being a target.

Years later, I learned from my female cousins that I wasn't as unique as I'd thought. For some, the uncles' names are the same, for some they are different, but for most of us, our stories and our misplaced shame is the same.

The playground scene is just one of many vivid memories I play repeatedly in my mind. When life

122

throws me a curveball, I remind myself of what I've endured, and I laugh and say cockily to the universe, "It's going to take a hell of a lot more than that to take me down!" Then I press on to the next challenge.

After the accidental death of my stepfather, my mother remarried and relocated us to Milwaukee, Wisconsin. My reprise from abuse was as short-lived as her second marriage. By the time I was nine, my mom had divorced and my worst nightmare had happened. Both my abusive uncles moved in with us.

This was when I stopped praying because it hurt less to believe that God didn't exist than to accept that he didn't care about me. Otherwise, why didn't he answer my prayers and make it stop?

The silver lining of moving North was that the higher quality Midwest educational system was a godsend, and I flourished in all things math- and computer-related. By eighth grade, I was no longer laboring every summer in the peanut and potato fields on my grandmothers' Louisiana farm; instead, I was enrolled in Marquette University's Upward Bound Pre-College program. Its full-time summer residency program and after-school and weekend classes kept me busy, challenged, academically focused, and, most importantly, away from home and safe from abuse.

My intellectual aptitude solidified my self-worth and by the time I was 14, I was well-read enough to know that I was not a victim and I had nothing to be ashamed of. My abusers' perversions were not mine! I refused to own their shame and I refused to allow anger to overtake me. And most significantly, I refused to let them win. I

123

would persevere, I would succeed, and I would triumph if for no other reason than to beat them. I was going to show them! I was going to be somebody great!

I was too stubborn and too strong to lose—I was *invincible*! Once I learned that word, I took it as my own. I wrote "invincible" on everything—doodling on notebooks, marking it on my lockers, inking my arm and hands, and printing and airbrushing it on T-shirts. Today INVINCIBLE is tattooed on my body and INVNCBL is my personalized license plate. As strong as I am, I still need visual reminders.

My other tattoos also empower me: *Stronger than yesterday, Legacy of my ancestors, No more excuses*, and *No one's victim*. Find the messages that inspire you and solidify the positivity you need to beat your own internal demons and accomplish your goals and dreams for your life. Write them down—or tattoo them!—and look at them often.

Failure was no longer an option . . .

Hard work and discipline earned me a coveted spot at Rufus King, the best public high school in my city. I graduated in the top of my class with multiple AP college credits and a full scholarship to Alverno College, and the best thing that ever happened to me—my one-month-old son. I'd kept my pregnancy a complete secret until my seventh month. I had good practice at keeping secrets and being invisible. I was already overweight, and between school, night, and weekend classes at Marquette and my part-time job at McDonald's, I was rarely home.

When I was ready to let my family know, I intentionally wore a less baggy sweatshirt and waited for all hell to break loose. And that's exactly what happened. My mother's immediate response was to slap me, spit on me, and cart me around to doctors unethical enough to perform a late-term abortion. Her biggest concern was not my health, mental nor physical, but how *she* was going to look to her church friends.

After refusing an abortion despite her threats, and despite the lack of formal prenatal care, I gave birth to a beautiful, healthy 9.5-pound baby boy. At my scheduled induction, I was 17 years old and still a minor, so I was at my mother's mercy. When the doctor asked her permission to give me an epidural during my prolonged labor, she said spitefully, "She should've thought about that when she opened her legs." At that moment, I knew I was on my own.

My first son's name is Demetric, and being the math nerd that I am, I love that he has *metric* in his name. Being the overthinker that I am, I love that the root of the meaning of his name is *measurement* because the standard of measure that mattered most since his birth was how good a mother I would be. One look into Demetric's innocent, dark brown eyes and I had more love for my son than I had for myself. We had each other and I was going to protect him. I wasn't sure what being a good mother looked like, but I would start by protecting him from everything that hurt me in my childhood. A huge part of my mental fortitude definitely comes from my desire to be a good mother—

there's nothing more important. Motherhood was my first lesson in selflessness.

I was forced to grow up fast. I stayed on my Aunt Lesley's couch for a while, then with help from my son's father, welfare, and the money I'd been saving in my "Run Away From Home Fund" since I was (literally) four years old, I rented and furnished my first apartment. I've been on my own ever since.

My new reality was that I was a welfare mother with a newborn son, a full-time college student at Alverno College, pursuing a double major in Applied & Abstract Mathematical Concepts and Computer Science and holding on to a full scholarship upon which my life literally depended. The choice was solely up to me— and not just for me, but for Demetric. I was going to either conquer or fail!

126

There was no time for self-pity nor self-doubt. I had a child to raise, dreams to manifest, plans to accomplish, and decisions to make.

My choices were clear. I could sleep or I could cry. I could bond with my child, care for him, and give him a great childhood, or I could yearn for the one that was stolen from me. I could study and dream about the future I was building for us, or I could fester in anger at the perverts who tried to destroy mine. We all have turning points in our lives where we make decisions that alter the trajectory of the rest of our lives. Some of us will recollect these moments with regrets and others as victories. The choice is ours!

My four years at Alverno were remarkable and life-altering. My admissions counselor, Ellen, and her husband Michael remain my lifelong mentors, and they went above and beyond to support me and ensure my success as both a student and mother. One of my happiest Alverno memories is of Michael teaching me to drive.

But my happiest moment from those four years is when my second son, Devan, arrived just before mid-terms during my senior year. He couldn't attend daycare until he was six weeks old, but I refused to miss classes, so I decided to take him to every class and each mid-term exam. The nuns at my Catholic college were remarkable. They learned my schedule, retrieved my baby before my first class, and kept him, often until the end of the school day. If I had not been recruited by Alverno, if they had not believed in me despite my teen pregnancy, if they had not encouraged the mental fortitude that I now proudly possess, I'm not sure where I'd be. I'm not even sure *who* I'd be. The nuns also renewed my faith in people and God.

The birth of 'The Curvy Boss™'

Despite a traumatic childhood, I've not only survived, but I've also thrived. I've achieved unprecedented career and financial success in the male-dominated field of information technology, predominantly in insurance, data science, and real estate. I've made history as the first African American woman in a position of leadership in the Information Technology departments at the insurance companies where I've been employed for the last three decades, and I have accomplished many historical firsts and accolades.

Now I am also accomplishing entrepreneurial success as the CEO and Founder of Curvy Boss™ Travel. However, second only to the success of my marriage and my children, I am most proud of my body of community service work, in a wide variety of organizations ranging from fighting financial illiteracy to fighting hunger and combating child sex trafficking and abuse. I serve as a role model in my Milwaukee-area community, where I am affectionately known and self-branded as "The Curvy Boss™." The name is an homage to a quote from my grandmothers' favorite actress, Mae West: "Women are like roads. The more curves they have, the more dangerous they are." I am full of those curves Mae West warns about, both physically and figuratively, making "Curvy Boss" a force with which to be reckoned.

I could've given up many times, and most would agree I would've been justified in doing so. Instead, I've learned that whatever we choose to focus on is what will grow, whether it's in our thoughts, our souls, our lives, or our futures.

Rather than planting and watering self-doubt, guilt, shame, hurt, the past, anger, and anxiety in our gardens, instead plant love, knowledge, prosperity, positivity, and forgiveness. Every Sunday morning, I spend a couple of hours in silence, thinking, meditating, strategizing, and planning, and I often journal the thoughts and epiphanies that my conscious decides I'm ready to embrace. I've been too cowardly to share these thoughts with others, trying to convince myself that they are for my own personal growth and development. Until now, that is!

The most enlightening discovery that has enabled my growth is the full and unconditional acceptance of myself. I cannot overstress the importance of loving yourself and believing in yourself. Something miraculous happens when you do. When you accept yourself, flaws included, they are no longer weapons that others can leverage against you, and any remaining feelings of shame subside. When you are no longer burdened with negativity, you are no longer obsessed with the need to be perfect in adulthood in an impossible attempt to undo the unspeakable tragedies you've survived in childhood. When you wholeheartedly love yourself, you invest in yourself! When you invest in yourself, you create a return on your investment for generations to come—financially, spiritually, and emotionally!

When I was 21 and walked across the stage to receive my diploma, I drew a permanent line in the sand, and from that moment on I have never been quiet, have never hesitated to speak up, and have never stopped advocating for the most vulnerable among us— our children.

Whenever I feel weak, I take myself back to my college graduation. I close my eyes and remember my strength. I remember how much I believed in myself at that moment and how much my Alverno family believed in me. I also think about my children and my grandchildren, and I remind myself that I can't give up now. Then I'm good to go. It's almost like driving into a gas station and filling up an empty tank.

Here's another rejuvenation secret that I'd like to share: Whenever you find your belief in yourself

129

depleted, it is time to pause and take inventory. If you focus solely on you and your own needs, you will always run out of energy and motivation. The broader picture—your children, your marriage, your extended family, the greater needs of society, and the innocents among us who need you to be strong for them will supply never-ending fuel—keeping you going so you can continue to give more of your talents and of yourself to others.

When I was small, weak, and unprotected, all I desperately wanted was one person to protect me—just *one*. Now I aspire to be that one for the next child who longs for protection because I see myself in that child. It's not enough for me to be successful and for my children to be safe; I need *all* children to be safe! As long as there are children who are not safe, I have work to do. *We* have work to do.

My Louisiana grandmother, Larcenia, whom I cherished beyond words, would often say, "What the world has for you *is for you*, and only you!" She did her best to instill within me the understanding that everything coming my way—every blessing, every financial milestone, every academic first, and every career accomplishment—was due to *me*, and I deserved it. It was hard to hold on to her message through the abuse, but now that I'm older and find myself sharing her words with my children, they are starting to resonate with me and grow in my heart and mind.

Believing that you deserve to be successful is a very powerful catalyst. Once you believe that you are worthy of success and deserve success, nothing and no one can stand in the way. *No one*, not even yourself! And nothing will bring more joy and worth to your own life than accomplishing your dreams and helping your fellow sisters do the same.

Recently, I followed my own advice and unburdened myself of a defense mechanism that I no longer need— my morbid obesity. For my entire life, I'd hidden behind my fat to maintain a protective shield of invisibility and used food to self-medicate. I knew I deserved better. Empowered and supported by a tribe of health-minded friends, I lost more than 100 pounds in two years. I'm still a Curvy Boss™, just a lot healthier (and smaller) than before.

To all my fellow Curvy Bosses: Hang in there! Persevere. I promise you will find your own INVINCIBLE within yourself. The world is yours for the taking!

Author's Notes

I describe myself as an entrepreneur, a debt-free diva, recovering perfectionist, a financial literacy advocate, a community service leader, a wife, and a mother. The "Curvy Boss" is how I'm known locally and in my international social media community. Logically, it made sense for me to launch my new partnership with iBuumerang as the CEO and Founder of Curvy Boss™ Travel and Curvy Boss™ VibeRides Ride Share.

My broad and deep community service résumé includes membership in NAACP, Milwaukee Urban League, Women in Technology, Girls Who Code, Toast Masters, Microsoft IT Advisory Council, and the National Association of Insurance Women (NAIW). I served as the multi-year Youth Protection advisor for Midwest District #6270 of Rotary International and the Community Service Club Advisor for the Interact\Key Club at King High School.

My degrees in Applied & Abstract Mathematical Concepts and Computer Science from Alverno College led me to unprecedented success in the male-dominated

132

field of information technology. As a Microsoft-certified IT professional and SQL database administrator, I currently work as the Principal Database and ETL Administrator in the Insurance & Spatial Solutions division of the international conglomerate CoreLogic, Inc. (GLGX). My 26 years of experience in insurance have made me an internationally acclaimed leader, speaker, and instructor for IAIP, The International Association of Insurance Professionals.

Helen, my partner of 11 years, and I live in Milwaukee, Wisconsin. We have four children and two grandchildren, Addy and Ari. Our sons, Demetric, Devan, and step-son Derrick, are successful college graduates, and our daughter, Dalicia, is a junior at the University of Minnesota with plans to become a pediatrician.

Contact Information

Email:	Therease@BeInvincible.net
	Info@CurvyBossTravel.com
Websites:	www.BeInvincible.net
	www.CurvyBossTravel.com
FaceBook:	Therease.Thompson.7
	BeInvincibleNOW
	CurvyBosses
	CurvyBossTravel
	CurvyBossRideShare
Twitter:	@TheCurvyBoss
Instagram:	@BeInvincibleNOW
	@CurvyBossTravel
	@CurvyBossRideShare
LinkedIn:	Therease Thompson

Chapter 12

Fight Trauma With Truth and Forgiveness

Maureen Felley

My first traumatic memory is from when I was two years old and my dad walked out of our lives. I can see the entire scene play out in my head.

My sister and I were standing near the front door of our rented home, with our dad kneeling by us. He was talking to us quietly, explaining that he could not stay. Our mom was standing a few feet away, glaring at him, screaming, "Get out! LEAVE!" Her eyes were wild. She ran into the kitchen and came back with the coffee pot.

Wham! She hit my father over the head, the glass percolator top flying across the room as blood spurted out of his head. She threw him a towel from a pile of clean laundry on the couch and shrieked, "Get the hell out!"

She later told us our father had died in a plane crash. We didn't see him again until after she died in childbirth 10 years later.

My mother suffered from schizophrenia, which was a widely misunderstood mental illness in the 1960s. I know I really didn't understand what she experienced until a couple of years ago when I listened to a Ted Talk from a schizophrenic woman. She revealed that, unlike the rest of us who dream crazy stuff while we sleep and forget most of it the next morning, her schizophrenia has her "dreaming" during the day. She sees things around her—scary people and scenarios that are not real. She described my mother's symptoms perfectly and helped me put my memories in perspective. *A Beautiful Mind*, the movie about John Nash, the famous mathematician with schizophrenia, also gave me insight into my mother's world.

> *My painful experiences taught me to surround myself with people who want to live a loving and peaceful life.*

Schizophrenia is a terrifying disease for everyone involved, and my siblings and I developed ways of coping with my mother's illness that colored every reaction in my life. Some of the choices I have made astound me. I would not be in the situation in which I am living now except for the grace of God.

My childhood held many life lessons for me. Of course, at the time I could not see how God was in every aspect of what went on in our family. I only saw chaos and confusion, but that's where I learned to survive by flying under the radar of my mother's disease. I had to be helpful, obedient, and as invisible as I could be. That way, whenever she had a psychotic episode, I might not be the target of her rages, imagined scenarios, or physical abuse. I could hide under my bed or run into the woods up the street from our house. I spent much of my time outside where I could escape quickly.

Her violence happened randomly, mainly when she was stressed. Usually, it had to do with our monthly welfare check not showing up, which sent her into a frenzied spiral of ranting, accusations, hearing voices, or claiming that someone was stealing our mail. Sometimes, she put us in the car and drove around to find the mailman, frantic to convince him to look in his pile again and find her welfare check. My brother David and I would sit in the car, pretending not to notice how crazy our mother was acting, while I felt a huge pit open in my gut.

That *pit in my gut* feeling has been part of me for as far back as I can recall. Even now, I get it whenever a trigger from the past—a smell, a song, an old cliché, or a person who reminds me of faces in my past—puts me back into that period of torment.

What does my pit feel like? It's a hole that cannot be filled, a nagging hunger that cannot be satiated with food. It does not go away unless I give it over to the God of my understanding.

My mom looked normal most of the time. She didn't smoke, do drugs, or drink, because those things were not ladylike in her opinion. She was very pretty and in decent shape, especially considering she had given birth to five children. Her only entertainment was her beat-up piano, and she was an awesome classical pianist, playing for hours on end. The only time I felt safe was when she was at the piano. Whenever I saw her sit down to play, I knew I had at least two hours free from false accusations, yelling, or fear.

She had a habit of hitting us kids in public. I grew up with that, and at the time, I thought it was normal. Not only did she have issues controlling her anger, but she constantly called the police, telling them that she was hearing voices coming from the furnace, attic, or wherever. When the police came, she told them about nonexistent people who were bothering us, like the car thieves who didn't actually *steal* the car but did something so it wouldn't start in the morning. Or the neighbors who used a giant magnet to pull her car down our sloping driveway in the winter just to upset her. Or the countless times she complained that my innocent brothers were saying evil things about her behind her back. Each time the police came, it was a colossal waste of their time. Their visits revealed the extent of her insanity, and how deeply she needed help.

Stress played a big part in triggering her episodes. Whenever Mom was in a situation she couldn't control, or something happened that deviated from her concept of reality, she would spiral into a crazed world from which there seemed to be no escape. After a few hours, she would either fall asleep or play her piano. None of us kids would try to reason with her; we would make ourselves scarce, realizing that whatever was going on had to run its course.

I became adept at being a "good girl" and changing who I was in order not to be the object of her fury. That was something that I had to learn how to undo decades later, something that I continue to work on every single day, even today: *to speak my truth and not to please people out of fear.*

Again, FEAR. There is that word, my oldest friend, the part of me that can still haunt me unless I practice handing it over to a Power Greater than myself—every single day, several times a day. The experiences I have lived through have become an asset in my life, and now I can discern what I am able to change, and what I am powerless over. I listen to my "gut."

Once in a while, mom would try to take us to church. Church seemed unfriendly; a place filled with judgmental souls. While it is true that Mom was usually talking to herself, I wonder why the worshippers didn't have any compassion for her or us kids. Sometimes the pastor would talk about sin and divorce and it would stress Mom. On what turned out to be our last Sunday at that church, she stood up during his sermon on divorce and shouted, "Stop persecuting me!" Of course, in a nanosecond, ushers grabbed us and escorted us out. A few of them tried to calm Mom down and reason with her, but it was hopeless. She was in the middle of an episode.

We were not welcomed back to that church, and we kids breathed a sigh of relief every Sunday morning that we no longer had to attend. So much for Christian love, kindness, and understanding. My church experience led me to believe religion was for perfect families, those with a mom and dad, and a normal life. Exactly what *was* a child supposed to "do for God" in order to receive the safety net of comfort, peace, and loving parents? What was my purpose in this confusing life that I could not figure out?

From a very early age, I was awakened in the night by panic attacks. Although I had no idea what they were, I thought I was dying of a heart attack. I would sit up in my bed, feel my racing heart, and run across the hallway to my mom's bed, though I knew better than to wake her or tell her what was happening. In the darkness, I would be comforted by the spirit of the One Who Knew Me Before I Knew Him. I would gently rock myself to sleep, and in the morning, everything seemed to be better.

To this day, I need nightlights in my bedroom. Total darkness is not something that I find soothing, and I'm sure this is due to the traumatic adventures we had at night. Mom would wake us youngest three kids, force us into the car, and race down back roads at what seemed to be 100 miles per hour, running stop signs and traffic lights, screaming that the FBI was chasing us with guns and they would kill us if they caught us.

I remember crouching on the floor of our old Packard, terrified I'd be shot to death, while my mother was shouting that they were gaining on us. After what seemed like hours, she'd drive home, claiming she "lost them," and put us to bed.

In the morning, whenever I'd tell my sister that I had a terrifying, realistic dream, she'd usually give me a blank look and mutter, "That wasn't a dream."

As incredible as it seems, we'd all pretend nothing had happened the night before. Mom would be playing her piano or doing laundry and none of us would say a thing.

Other things happened in the middle of the night that weren't quite as dangerous but left me feeling confused and not in control, thinking that somehow, I deserved whatever happened, that I had been "bad" and was responsible for what transpired. As a child, I had long blond, straight hair. I never kept it brushed because I was a tomboy—a tree-climbing, running, and-playing-kickball kind of girl. Mom didn't like my untidy hair.

I sat up in bed one morning and my sister stared at me from across the room. "Oh, wow," she yelled, "what happened to your hair?"

"What? What are you talking about?" I jumped out of bed and looked into the mirror on the dresser next to my bed. My hair had been chopped off, raggedly butchered in the night. Apparently, Mom had decided to give me the home haircut that she thought I needed.

One early summer evening was a key moment in my childhood. The neighbors had called the police after watching my mom abuse us one too many times. I heard the police arrive at the front door, then I heard her start to cry and beg, "What about my babies? There is no one here to take care of them. I'm a single mom; I *can't* go with you."

I ran to the front of the house so I could see what was going on. There were two police cars and at least three policemen. Mom's handcuffed image is forever burned into my mind, and I can see the police almost dragging her down the hilly front yard. Terrified and confused, I hoped that maybe the police would help our mom by taking her to the doctors, and, after a few days, she would come back to us, healed and normal.

That was not what happened.

The next day, the shock hit, and I spent the morning on my bed crying. I was startled when my friend Dina's mother came into my room and sat next to me. She said gently, "Tell me what happened, Maureen." I cried even harder. Though I can't remember many of Mrs. Worden's words, I remember feeling the warm caring, unconditional love of God spilling out all over me. As I look back on my life, I know I experienced a God-inspired moment with Mrs. Worden. That is where my future zigged instead of zagged, where a detour changed the course of my life.

142

Child Protective Services dropped the ball. There were never any formal papers written up about us children, and we remained outside the system. Mrs. Worden took Donna, David, and me into her home for what she thought would be a few days until our mom came back. Little did she imagine that it would be almost six months. My older brothers stayed at our house. They were 16 and 17 with summer jobs, and Mr. and Mrs. Worden thought that they would be able to keep up the house so we would have a place to return to once mom got home.

The Wordens found a lawyer to work pro bono for Mom, and she was home after six months despite the doctors insisting she remain in the hospital. I remember feeling the pit in my stomach again, knowing life had been better when she was hospitalized.

Once home, Mom took herself off all the medications that had been prescribed for her schizophrenia, including Thorazine, and the results were disastrous. Hospital therapists had told her that she was lonely and needed male companionship (or so she said), so she began to date, at least until she became obviously pregnant. On February 18, 1972, Mom died of an embolism two days after delivering a baby boy. Because she refused to identify the father, the baby went into the adoption system. We met him for the first time 46 years later.

The Wordens took us in again, and we were contentedly settling back in with them when we got another shock. Dad was alive! CPS found him in California, and he was forced to return to Syracuse to care for us. Within five months we also had a stepmother who had several children of her own, and we were living in an unfamiliar town. Almost everything I'd known was gone, and I was living with volatile, unfriendly strangers. My new life was somehow more miserable and even less comprehensible than my old one.

I lived so much of my childhood in fear and confusion, and with little control. I was a small adult, worrying over the same worries that grownups had. Looking back at the fear and rage I had as a child, I'm astounded, and I'm sure my nighttime panic attacks were a direct result.

My fears were many. I would wonder if our house would get struck by lightning every time it rained. When it got dark outside, I feared *everything*. I could not allow myself to depend on any person, because I was not sure what they would do. I feared people, places, and things,

143

because I did not have a clear understanding of where I fit in, or with whom.

However, even as a young child, I found other people's problems fascinating, and *always* made them my business. That way, maybe I could "help" by offering encouragement, advice, or a suggestion that could somehow take away the pain of others. I had taken on every other person's pain, thinking that I could fix them.

These are the same themes in my life today. I still am a people-pleaser, in need of control, who finds it hard to mind her own business, still focusing on other people's problems and trying to fix them so I can feel better.

That is why I continue to follow a twelve-step program to learn to take care of myself rather than focus on other people's problems. I have spent a great deal of energy learning to focus on myself instead because *I* am more than I can handle. My twelve-step program saved my life. It also introduced me to a Higher Power that showed me the truth. Granted, it took me 53 years to get there, but my life and my personality all make sense now. I now realize I had tried to please God with my actions and deeds so He would love me. When I was a child, I had no idea there was such a thing as unconditional love.

I've learned I need to accept the truth of what transpired in my life and use it as my motivation to improve myself, to work harder in every way. The trauma of my childhood drove me to search for healing through counselors, prayer, and my twelve-step program. My painful experiences taught me to surround myself with people who want to live a loving and peaceful life.

144

We do not have to allow our pasts to pave a future of pain and bitterness. Instead, I used my past to bring me to a healthier way of life. I have empathy, discernment, wisdom, and the ability to see humor in almost anything, gifts that I would not have received without my childhood experiences.

My life today is an ongoing journey as I continue to learn how to be a better human being and how to forgive with the help of Jesus Christ.

Author's Notes

I've worked since I was 11 years old: as a nanny while still a young teenager, in restaurants, as a counselor at a detention center, and as an office supplies salesperson before becoming a stay-at-home mother. I have volunteered for several charities, including a resource center for pregnant women who plan to keep their children.

146

I grew up in upper New York State and attended Cazenovia College, which was, at the time, an all-women's college. I moved to Texas in 1989. My husband Brian and I have a blended family of three daughters, two sons, and ten grandchildren. We reside in the Dallas-Ft. Worth area.

Contact information

Email: MaureenFelley@gmail.com

Chapter 13

Stand Up For Yourself!

Kenny Wynn

When I sit down and recall the events in my life and the decisions I made that led me to where I am today, they almost seem like they are part of someone else's life. I think to myself, *There's no way I did all of that.*

I consider myself blessed and highly favored by God to have had the chance to experience everything I have in my life to date. Some experiences were not so good, and many I don't care to recall, but all have helped mold me into the man I am still becoming. I discovered I have a passion for serving, coaching, and educating others to help them achieve their goals and dreams.

At first, this didn't seem like a passion, but more of a necessity.

I grew up in a Christian home with a ton of love and fantastic childhood memories. My upbringing was almost too good because when I left home for college and stepped into the adult world, I was shocked. I quickly learned that I knew nothing of the real world and even less about myself. Up until that point, everything I needed had been provided for me or I'd just worked a bit to earn it, clueless to what was required of me in order to thrive and survive in the world.

When I left to attend college at the University of North Texas in Denton, Texas, I was finally away from mom and dad and free to make my own choices and decisions.

Just take the time to know yourself, speak from your experiences, pay attention to the lessons you've learned, and trust yourself.

At first, my only motivation was happy hours, house parties, the men's lacrosse team, and the occasional visit to my classes. To help with expenses, I needed a job, and I found one in the service industry right away.

My career began with slinging margaritas and 99-cent Enchilada Wednesdays. At the time, I was happy to have a job and I enjoyed being a part of people's guilty pleasures of Tex-Mex food. Working as a waiter and bartender, my eyes opened to what I call my passion: *service.* I enjoyed the service industry so much that

I decided to make it my field of study. So, like every American college student, I changed my major.

When I started studying Hospitality Management, I began to develop a real relationship with the business and structure of serving others. In the service industry, you learn much more than wine varietals, food specials, and how to make a Vegas Bomb. The industry forces you to come out of your shell and demands that you interact. It makes you smile when a smile is not warranted, often finding tactful ways to tell people *no* or that their card is declined without saying the dread words. The service industry is a constant reminder that the world is full of great and fantastic people—and also full of cruel and evil individuals you must deal with every day.

Serving others will, without a doubt, force you to know yourself in a way that will carry you through many different challenges and unique situations for the rest of your life. At one point, I worked the bar at night clubs and upscale restaurants where people freely shared their stories with me; often I'd be asked to solve problems or give advice. During this stretch of dealing with drunks, addicts, and overall decent people, I began to see myself and the direction of my life much more clearly.

Once I genuinely knew myself and was able to project confidence (even though I was still constantly second-guessing myself), doors began to open. I was a busboy, a barback, a dishwasher, then a supervisor, soon floor/service manager, next general manager, consultant, operations manager, and eventually a business owner.

Every one of those titles and responsibilities came from simply knowing myself, paying attention to lessons learned, and trusting myself throughout the process—even when I was wrong. I spent 12 years in the service industry refining my craft and putting other people's needs in front of my own.

Like all things in life, change and the ability to adapt is necessary in order to survive. A change for me was an absolute must after those dozen years. Burnout was setting in. In my opinion, many people were taking advantage of my well-developed skills to suit their needs, leaving me with scraps.

My wake-up call came when my best client, a man who represented 80% of my income, decided he no longer needed my services and was moving in a different direction. This betrayal caused me to spiral out of control, internally. My career was built on serving people and helping them reach their goals in many ways. Working with celebrities and high-net-worth individuals made me feel as though I had reached my own goals, when, in reality, I was just one contract or one client away from failure. As much as I'd learned about myself and my passion for serving others, it wasn't enough for me to feel purposeful or accomplished in a healthy and sustainable way.

It dawned on me that I'd been helping *others* find success, and my happiness all came from that. I'd become content with living off the crumbs and scraps of those that I choose to work with, and all my energy was helping them grow their visions. Unfortunately, I was not taking care of *me* and *my* needs. I wasn't replenishing my mental resources.

When I realized that, yes, I was upset. Fortunately, I also became motivated to live my own life, to never again allow someone else to choose my priorities and control my actions.

This insight encouraged me to stand up for myself and own my worth, skills, and talent. I finally understood we need to trust ourselves and reference our past experiences, individual victories and failures, learn from our heartbreaks, and embrace personal growth from lessons we learned.

By 2019, I'd been working for myself in financial services and business-to-business sales for four years. While I still loved serving and coaching others to help them achieve their goals, I was in control of my own earning potential and I had the ability to guide and help people in a different way.

It was time for a change. I launched my small business concierge service at two key urban areas in Texas, Dallas-Ft. Worth and Austin. Then I partnered with American Teacher Retirement Services, an organization that allowed me to grow my book of business with teachers and educators throughout the state of Texas. The partnership also gave me an opportunity to grow a team of other like-minded individuals, all of whom I trained and assisted in the growth of their own personal business.

The business was growing and things looked great because I was developing a decent client list. I enjoyed my time serving them, making sure that all their needs were met to the best of my abilities. I was still doing what I am passionate about, which is serving others.

On paper, my professional life was gaining momentum and my team was finding success as well.

Sadly, my personal life was not doing nearly as well. I was at least 50 pounds overweight, drinking a bit more than usual, and mending a broken heart from a failed relationship. My debts and doubts were looming, and my confidence was cratering. Apparently, there was no cure for the fog of discontent that followed me around. Though I knew I found peace when I helped or served others, really what I needed was someone to help *me.*

Pretty quickly, I discovered nobody was coming to help me. *I* needed to get up, I needed to serve myself. I needed to do something that, *one*, would get me out of this rut, and *two*, would continue to move forward after the rut was behind me.

I'll never forget that decisive moment in my life: I was sitting in my truck in a random parking lot, in tears, thinking about what I should do next, and how to deal with the noise in my head and pain in my heart. On the radio, a commercial for the Army National Guard was talking about making a difference. I heard the spokesmen speak about lifestyle change and new beginnings. They mentioned serving local communities and fellow Americans nationwide. It was like one of those scenes in a movie when the person begs, *God! Give me a sign!* and then there's *Boom, here's your sign!*

So I called the number and made an appointment with the recruiter on the spot. A sense of peace came over me. I've always believed that God has a plan for me and my life, and if I simply put my faith in his wisdom and stop trying to control everything around me, I could see more clearly and be able to receive the blessings that are laid out for me.

The Army offered to help me pay off my student loans, giving me freedom from debt sooner rather than later. They gave me a great signing bonus, and many other military and VA benefits that will be instrumental to aid me and my future family one day. Joining the Army gave me a purpose again and is shaping me into the next version of myself—the 2.0 better version.

Days after my commitment, doubts began to set in: *I'm old, I'm fat and out of shape, and what will happen if I fail? What will people say? I'm going to struggle being the oldest person at basic combat training . . . will my body hold up? Will they break me mentally?* I had so many questions, *so* many doubts, and many times I was close to backing out. But I had made up my mind to find success and live a life of my design; I had promised myself to trust the process of growth and change. Trust yourself.

On August 23, 2019, I enlisted in the Texas Army National Guard. Almost exactly two months later, I shipped off to basic training at the ripe old age of 33.

Boot camp was a challenge. At first, I was too nervous to say or do anything. It was as though I'd forgotten about all I've been through and everything that had brought me to that moment. Drill sergeants at least a decade younger than I am were screaming at me, telling me what to do, disrespecting my intelligence, treating me like a worthless piece of garbage. I seemed to be surrounded by young juvenile delinquents, over-sensitive mama's boys and girls, and spoiled little brats. They were everywhere. I was sure I had nothing in

153

common with an 18- to 25-year-old at this point in my life. *C'mon!* One girl didn't even know who the Fresh Prince of Bel-Air was! Seriously! I felt really outdated.

Every day was a struggle for me during those first few weeks. Waking up early, working out before the sun was up, doing ungodly numbers of push-ups and sit-ups was quite the adjustment. Also, being away from friends and family was a drag. There was no one around to call a friend, and I had little in common with those who were available and willing to talk with me.

Then one day, something changed inside me. We were getting a corrective adjustment in the form of intense physical activities, for what seemed like forever. I finally noticed that everyone around me was suffering, just the same as I was. I noticed I wasn't the only one sweating and struggling. I was not the only one who wanted to stop and go home. It made me think about all the other things I've overcome and dealt with. It made me consider all the thousands of people in the world who deal with way worse problems. I realized how fortunate I was to have the opportunity to *be* there. Many people who want to join the service can't, due to illness, bad life choices, or heredity issues beyond their control.

Soon I discovered the physical training wasn't so punishing anymore.

I finally began to trust myself, lean on faith, and recall the many lessons I'd learned to date. When I was placed in several leadership roles, I realized my chain of command clearly saw something in me that I hadn't yet realized I had. During both Basic and Advanced Individual Training, I was appointed squad leader and platoon guide. I was forced to give orders and make decisions on behalf of my fellow soldiers and had to represent those soldiers to the higher ranks by serving as their voice. These leadership roles came as a surprise, and they were more rewarding than I expected.

Never underestimate how powerful and capable you can be.

Mentally, I knew they couldn't break me because my foundation was strengthened by years of trials and errors. My age and wisdom only served as a bonus, because I was able to give wise counsel to my younger battle buddies. I was before I realized it, ready, and already groomed for this challenge.

Though I don't intend to go "active duty" in the military, which means full-time, I do plan to go to Officer Training School soon. I intend to become the leader many of these soldiers need. There's a great need for strong leadership within Army ranks, and during my experiences in the service, I've learned that I've always had what it takes to qualify.

The Army made me into a stronger, much more confident man, and I have new skills and traits I can use to support myself and my future family. I have realized I can do *anything*, just as long as I am willing to put out the effort.

Often life presents a challenge that seems too big to tackle or we just aren't equipped to manage. The truth is you *are* ready for it! Life has been preparing you for each milestone that you reach. It's a matter of whether you believe you can do it and are willing to do whatever it takes—*never quitting*—to make it to the finish line.

Taking these few steps has made me a better servant to others—mainly because *I* am no longer in the way. I plan to keep learning and sharing my experience so others don't need to make the same mistakes I did.

My story is similar to the story of many of you who are out there looking for answers and guidance. Just take the time to know yourself, speak from your experiences, pay attention to the lessons you've learned, and trust yourself.

If you have been following me down my previous mistake-ridden path of inertia and lack of confidence, don't worry, it *all* works in your favor once you choose to change.

Author's Notes

During my initial Army training, I dropped close to 30 pounds and I am much stronger and more fit. Both my weight loss and my physical condition boosted my overall confidence, and I'm doing my best to maintain the new changes in my mental and physical strength. Consistency is the key to maintaining all positive growth, in my opinion.

The year 2020 brought uncertainty and the infamous coronavirus. Most of my business and way of life have been deemed nonessential services and are not in demand. Tomorrow is not guaranteed to be a repeat of today, so the ability to learn new skills is important for survival. The Army has taught me to be an electrician, and my new skill is the financial life preserver that got me through the pandemic. I'll continue to develop different skill sets and develop traits that will become the safety net for me and my future.

I was born in San Antonio, the only boy with two sisters, and people say I was spoiled by my parents (I can't argue with that!). I received my B.S. in Hospitality Management from the University of North Texas in Denton, and now I live in Dallas. Having lived my entire life in Texas, I'd be excited to travel and live in a variety of places around the world. I still own the concierge business, but we are not taking new clients or doing any transactions until the chaos of the pandemic passes and I rebrand the business.

Keep your eyes and ears out for my next project!

Contact information

Email:	ConnectWithKennyWynn@gmail.com
Website:	http://Kennywynn.now.site
Facebook:	Kenny Wynn
Instagram:	@Kenwynn08
Twitter:	@Connectw_KennyW
Snapchat:	Kenwynn08

Chapter 14

Your Perception
Changes Everything

Deirdre Goveia

*When you change the way you look at things,
the things you look at change.*

Wayne Dyer

I sit here today in total awe of my life and the
overwhelming love I have in my heart. I want to
share my journey with others so that they too can
use their pain to heal, let go, and experience the state
of bliss I've come to know. I don't believe anyone should
wait to live their best life. The gratitude I feel to all
the people and situations (good and bad) that helped
me get to where I am today, I can't put a price on, and I
wouldn't change one thing.

I could tell you painful sad stories of my life, but to be honest, when I look back, I realize my life was exactly the way it was meant to be. I believe everyone was doing the best they could. I have been blessed by every experience and would not change a thing. I also admit my memories are just *my* perception of how things were because each of us sees life through a different lens.

> *We all have the same opportunities because true success comes from having the right mindset.*

The magical shift in my perception started December 21, 2010, and my entire life has evolved in the decade since. Life is a precious gift, today and every day. Do I still have challenges? Yes, but now I know how to see and use every single experience as an opportunity for growth.

It wasn't always like this, though. My self-loathing, self-abuse, drinking, guilt, blaming, anger, and resentment had escalated over the years. I hated myself; I wanted out!

When I look back 15 years, my life was a mess. I was in pain and filled with self-pity. My marriage was a total disaster, I blamed my husband for everything, constantly ran from my pain, and looked for anything to numb it. When I found temporary relief, usually through alcohol, I hated myself even more, because I always needed more to fill that empty feeling again and again. Nothing could make me feel better, and my anger and resentment grew when I drank. I'd become a stranger to myself, a person I didn't like anymore. I was on a slippery slope, and deep down I knew it.

My heart broke when Ralph, our only son, asked if he could go to boarding school. Though I was devastated, my husband and I agreed, and the decision was a good one. He blossomed being away at school.

In June 2010, my dad passed away, and I used that grief to escalate my drinking to another level. My "excuse" was that Mom needed company, a drinking buddy, so I would go and have a glass of wine with Mom every evening and end up finishing a bottle, maybe two. For six months, I drank daily and found myself getting angrier and becoming more and more resentful of life.

On December 21, 2010, I finally hit bottom when Ralph was home for Christmas holidays. After a 15-hour drinking binge with friends, I woke up with no memory of the night before, staring into the face of my beautiful son. The fear, disappointment, and sadness were so clear behind the tears in his big blue eyes.

A flashback seared me: As a child, I promised myself I would never be a parent like mine became when they drank, yet I had. Something in me shifted that moment: *This cannot go on.* I was hurting the person who meant the most to me in this world. It had to stop.

The decision I made that morning changed my life forever.

Was it easy? No, but I knew it was my only choice. I'd always wanted things to change, but I was looking in the wrong place. I wanted my husband to love me, to treat me better, to show me I was worthy. I thought if *he* changed, I would be happy. But it wasn't *his* job. It was mine.

A few years earlier I had been given a copy of *The Power of Now,* a book written by Eckhart Tolle. I'd tried to read it, but I wasn't ready to surrender my victim mentality and hear his message. I don't believe in coincidences because I feel all is divinely orchestrated for our highest good, so it's ironic *The Power of Now* caught my eye that momentous day (I swear it was actually calling my name). I picked it up and read it again, and this time I was ready. The message was so clear.

I ran to my husband's workshop, shouting, "Ronnie, I've got it! I've got it! It isn't your fault, it's mine!" He didn't have a clue as to what I meant; our relationship was so bad at that stage, we hardly communicated at all. I knew I needed space to try to understand life and my part in it.

162   I moved out of the house and into a small cottage on our property, living alone, and totally submerging myself in personal development. I absorbed works from teachers including Abraham Hicks, Louise Hay, Wayne Dyer, Eckhart Tolle, Gregg Braden, Bruce Lipton, and Guy Finley. After six months, I moved back into our house, and I continued taking online courses, reading books, and watching DVDs. All these great teachers gave me the same message: *We create our own reality. No one out there is to blame for anything.*

This was such an exciting revelation; a feeling of freedom came over me as I accepted the message. After several years of studying, I took a transformational life coaching course in South Africa and became fully immersed in spiritual teachings and personal development. My life continued to improve as I took more responsibility for my life and did my best not to blame others.

Is that easy to do? *No*, but like anything in life, you just keep practicing.

My passion is to share what I have learned during the last 10 years. If I can start to change at the age of 46, anyone can.

As humans, we are so needy for things to fulfill us, to make us feel better about ourselves—and we are all looking in the wrong place. We are looking from the outside in rather than the inside out. We desperately need to shift our focus.

I write this chapter in late March 2020, in the early months of a global pandemic. Though it's a harsh reality, the world situation is an opportunity for us to reflect, bring our focus back to ourselves. The universe is always responding to us, and if we come from a place of fear, we attract more fear. This is a time for us to look at our relationship with life, come back to reconnecting with our hearts, and connect with love.

When I think about the time when I was so unhappy, I remember feelings of emptiness, hopelessness, and helplessness; and that is exactly where we are as a planet. I remember thinking, *"What can fix this and make it better; who can help me?"* When I finally realized *nothing* and *no one* out there could help, everything began to shift.

I understood the only change I needed was to change my perception of life—both the way I show up every day and my own attitude.

This is what we all need to do.

We fear everything is going to run out, so we think we need more control, more wealth, more *things*. However, the world is our mirror, and as every spiritual text tells us, we are made in His likeness. We must ask ourselves, what does that leave out? *We* are the creators of our reality; *we* are all manifestations of consciousness—of God. We already have all we need within each of us.

If that is true—and it is!—can you imagine the power we each have within us to BE the change? We have been looking at life from a perspective of fear, focused only on the negative, on what we lack, on what we don't like. Every time we reject a moment, we are rejecting ourselves and we are rejecting God. We are rejecting an opportunity for growth.

Imagine that every day you moan and complain about your life, your body, and how you don't like it, and how you resent others for what they have and you don't. Are you operating from a mindset of abundance or fear? *Fear.*

Remember, you reap what you sow. The universe/consciousness/God responds to our vibrations, and it will show you more situations to match your fearful vibration.

Our experience is our mirror to everything we see in the world just as everything we see in the world is a reflection of what is going on inside of us. *We* need to change. *We* need to take responsibility and stop blaming governments, our partners, the traffic, our upbringing, our race, and our circumstances.

Instead, we need to look at ourselves, each one of us, and ask, *How am I showing up? When I show up, do I look at people with fear, with a lack of trust, doubt, judgment, and resistance, or can I show up being the best version of me, looking at everybody as my equal, everyone and everything as a reflection of me, everything from a place of love and compassion, not judgment and criticism?*

Since I've been more conscious of my perception of life, I've discovered that the world, *my world*, has drastically changed for the better. Even in the midst of fear, I have the capacity to meet the situation and make use of it for my personal growth. We all can do this.

I would like to share a couple of amazing experiences.

One day I was in a grateful, happy mindset, heading to the airport to collect a friend, taking my usual shortcut through an impoverished neighborhood—when I saw an overwhelmingly lovely sight. The road ahead rose up a hill like a silvery river, and each side was lined with gold—beautiful, tiny orange flowers. I was in awe of this beauty; it actually took my breath away.

165

I collected my friend, and she was not in a happy place. The entire trip back from the airport, she ranted, raved, blamed, and complained about life. We came to the intersection with the beautiful silver road, I turned to go down the hill past the flowers, and she blurted, "What is wrong with people, why can't they throw their rubbish in the right place? Look at this road!"

It was like being slapped across the face. I was in total shock. Where were the beautiful flowers? I, too, could only see the trash! This hit me like a ton of bricks. Where had the flowers gone? How could this be? Only 50 minutes ago I felt so much love and appreciation for this beautiful road, this gilded vision, and now it was gone. What had happened? Had it been real?

I had allowed my level of consciousness, my perception of life, to be influenced by her lower emotional state, her level of consciousness. I'd allowed myself to sink to her level. The amazing life lesson I learned was this: *Reality is individual.* Reality is personal and totally dependent on your level of consciousness at any given moment.

Looking through loving eyes, you can only be met with love from whatever you focus on. Looking at someone or something with kindness and compassion, you are going to see kindness and compassion. Looking with judgment and resentment, you will be met with the same. Everything is our mirror.

If we understand that, then every moment of the day shows us how well we are doing or where we need to work on ourselves and our perception of life. We must stop being so hard on ourselves. Instead, we need to embrace everything that comes into our experience, including the emotions that come up when we are triggered. When we see something we don't like, we need to embrace it and realize that everything out there is a gift.

A second revelation: All suppressed emotions are guaranteed to resurface eventually. I learned not long ago that I hadn't dealt with some negative emotions from my past—I had only buried them. When a friend of mine told me she was leaving her husband, I felt like I had been hit by a truck. The painful feelings that bubbled up in my chest were memories of my past. I was jealous of her freedom, feeling resentment like I have never felt before.

166

Understand, my current life is happy, so my visceral reaction was way out of proportion to what I felt. That moment, I realized my friend had given me a gift. Her news had unlocked the unconscious negative energy, it was time to let it go. We are always being presented with opportunities to heal old hurts, so we must pay better attention to ourselves. Our bodies are always talking to us, looking for opportunities to release the negative energy we unconsciously store within us.

It's my belief that most disease is caused by unconscious negative emotions (energy) we've suppressed. To stay as healthy as possible, I use a great little technique: Just observe your emotional state and talk to it. Repeat *I love you, I accept you, and I let you go*, repeatedly from your heart, until the feeling disappears. And it will.

If we want to see change, we need to be aware of *our* perception. *Be the change you want to see.* The Wayne Dyer quote at the beginning of the chapter says it best: *When you change the way you look at things, the things you look at change.*

That is the truth. It covers absolutely every aspect of our lives. The key to that truth, though, is that we must look from our *hearts*, not our heads. Humanity has lost connection with our hearts. We have become so focused on external stimulation that we live in our heads, constantly judging and comparing. We've forgotten to listen to our hearts. Everything from our heads is *ego* and everything from our hearts is *truth*—our higher self.

The world has been presented with a gift that can shift us all back to connecting with our hearts. Nothing out there needs to change, *we* need to change. We need to look at each other with compassion and love, not judgment and fear. We need to understand that we are all magnificent, and we each have a gift to offer in our lifetime. We need to see that we are all living cells of the same living organism, EARTH. Every single one of us counts; we all have a purpose.

My purpose is to share my message with people here in Zambia and throughout the world. We all have the same opportunities because true success comes from having the right mindset. The attitude with which we meet the world every morning is where our power lies. Yes, our stories and circumstances often delay or make it more difficult to change. I'm empathetic because it took me 46 years before I made the choice to change. Now my mission is to show others they too can change and reach their full potential no matter what the circumstances.

Each day I wake up and set an intention to be a better version of myself than I was the day before. Do I achieve this every day? No, but I do most days, and that's what counts.

I look at my amazing son, Ralph, my angel, who saved my life. His wisdom is way beyond his years, and I've learned so much from him. As a six-year-old, his dream was to be in the Olympics, and he made it, representing Zambia at the 2016 Rio Olympic games. He has done nothing but make my husband and me proud. I look forward to watching him on his spiritual journey. I believe he is a teacher and is already making a difference in the lives of others.

My husband and I are now in the best place we have ever been, and I am grateful for our relationship every day.

We all need to know that if we want love we must be loving *first*, if we want kindness, we must be kind *first*, if we want respect, we must be respectful *first*.

It all starts with you! **Change is a choice**. Find grace in everything and absolutely anything is possible.

Author's Notes

Born in England to Irish parents, Deirdre has lived in Lusaka, Zambia since she was three years old. She owns Conscious Living, a life-coaching business, providing motivational speaking, online coaching, one-on-one coaching, and group workshops.

Deirdre and her husband Ronnie have been married for 27 years. Their son Ralph lives in South Africa,

where he is finishing his degree in sound engineering and swims competitively worldwide. Deirdre's mother, Una McDonough, a physical education and swimming instructor, inspired Ralph to start swimming competitively at six years old. He represented Zambia at the 2016 Olympics and is in training for the 2021 Olympics.

Contact Information:

Email: deirdregoveia@gmail.com
Facebook: Conscious Living – Deirdre Goveia
Instagram: @deirdregoveia
LinkedIn: @Deirdre Goveia
WhatsApp: +260966842132

Chapter 15

What *Do* You Have?

Melissa Monts

I magine yourself on a deserted island. No modern-day conveniences. No tools to work with. No ability to communicate with the outside world.

You look around and begin to assess your immediate needs: food, shelter, and water. Next, you begin to assess the available resources. After that, it's time to assess yourself: What skills, abilities, or talents do you have at your disposal?

Little by little, you put your survival plan together. Between the resources you find and your innate skills, you manage to hold on until you're rescued.

That is what I mean by *what do you have.*

Most of us don't think this way. We are trained to always think of what we *don't* have, what we lack. We are not taught to take inventory of ourselves and our circumstances and proceed with what we have. We are told to get more education, make more money, or get more experience. Rarely are we ever told to use what we have right now, right where we are.

But even if it goes against our life-long training, this is what we must learn to do if we are going to create mental wealth.

> *On my journey to mental wealth, I learned I had to return to my past so that I could recover from my childhood trauma.*

This concept was a very integral part of my recovery from mental illness. I had to learn how to take inventory of where I had been and learn to use it to get me where I wanted to go.

Poisoned roots

"Go ahead and eat it yourself, you fat pig, you know you want it." "You're fat, black, and nappy-headed; nobody wants to hear what you have to say." "Go sit your fat behind down somewhere and stop rubbing yourself all over married men." These are just some of the hurtful words that were hurled at me every day as I grew up.

I wasn't really "raised." I was the oldest of four, and no one taught me about grooming, how to clean or be organized. I was consistently thrown into situations with no preparation, and expected to figure it out myself.

When I didn't figure it out, I was heavily punished or brutally criticized.

When I was two, it was cute that I could eat an adult-size plate of food. But when I was ten, I was a "fat slob eating everybody out of house and home." When we were weighed in fifth-grade gym class, everyone saw I was a whopping 150 pounds. At first, I thought it was cool that I weighed more than all the other kids. That good feeling didn't last long, just until the other kids called me names. When I got home, my family both laughed at me and blamed me for eating all the time.

I was raped—many times. I was told the assaults were my fault. Even at just 10, I thought the only reason I'd been put on this earth was to please a man. Why did I keep letting it happen? I didn't realize I was doing what I was taught to do when I was three years old.

173

I have always been able to remember that I was raped for the first time as a toddler. I was told to keep quiet and endure the pain. That made me a good little girl. This went on for about two years. It wasn't until I was grown that I realized I was actually being trafficked.

When I broke my silence and admitted I remembered what happened to me at three, I became the black sheep of the family, a bad seed that had to be destroyed and uprooted. As if the abuse that I was already enduring wasn't enough, I now had to bear the brunt of fury in addition to carrying the load of being the oldest child.

The worst part was the toll it took on me mentally. I felt worthless, unwanted, unneeded, and I struggled with suicidal thoughts. After I got a horrific beating with a stick like a baseball bat, I wrote a note to God, asking Him to take me now if this was what life was going to be like. It was my first suicidal moment, and I was only 10 years old.

That was also the year a retired police officer raped me. At 13, it was my step-uncle.

The remainder of my childhood was very tumultuous and chaotic. I was in a swirl of constantly darting, slashing insults and abuse, struggling mentally to survive. I was never pretty enough. I was never fast enough. I was never smart enough. I was never kind enough. I am not sure how I made it through those years.

Twisted development

I was thrust into adulthood totally unprepared. I had dropped out my senior year, and after I found out I was pregnant, I re-enrolled, determined to graduate, and taking my senior year over again. My daughter was born before the end of the school year, on March 31, when I had just turned 19. When I had her, I realized for the first time what it was to feel love, to have a full heart. It was a foreign feeling.

Though I was taking my classes at home, I was required to go to school to take some supervised tests. My little girl went to school for the first time when she was just a couple of weeks old, riding with me on the school bus, strapped into her car seat.

The idea of moving away from home was something I looked forward to, something I'd imagined for years. At the same time, I was afraid of living alone and having to make it on my own, especially with a young child.

The decision was made for me when I was kicked out of the house after a fight over how to parent my daughter. That was pretty ironic considering my family's tradition of dysfunction. I was told to pack my things and my daughter and I were dropped off in nearby Oklahoma City the next day.

The Salvation Army homeless family shelter was the only place I could find to stay on such short notice. Initially, I was frightened but this feeling soon waned, and a brand new feeling of freedom took its place. Even though a room at the shelter was not an ideal starting place, I was away from all the chaos, criticism, and ridicule. I was finally free to call my own shots, to make my own way.

Within a month, I had my first apartment through the local Housing Authority. Again my fears returned. I had never lived in public housing, which was also known as the Projects, and I felt very vulnerable. Once again I overcame my fear rather quickly; I was in my own space and I could make my own rules.

I wanted so badly to do things so differently and give my child so much better than what I had gone through. But I still battled a very negative thought pattern. The belief that all I was good for was to lie down for a man was still with me. It didn't take long before I had a son. I wasn't married and his father and I were no longer speaking by the time he was born. Somehow it felt different to be raising a boy without a father; I had no idea how to raise a boy alone. My anxieties and my fears for my son's well-being never seemed to leave my mind.

As I struggled to keep our housing, keep working, and go to school, my thoughts about myself remained the same. My low self-esteem and lack of direction only added to my challenges. I constantly thought to myself *there's got to be a better way*. I just didn't know how to find it.

I had my third child by the time I was 27 years old. I had at least married her father, though that marriage was very short-lived, not to mention my most abusive relationship to date. Someone told me that one of the church leaders had preached about me, saying that I had gotten married just long enough to get pregnant again.

All the negativity, chaos, and abuse I'd absorbed my whole life was carried over into my own parenting. Because I was so overwhelmed and still struggling with the pain from my own childhood, I passed some of that pain on to my own children. I had no clue about the damage I was doing to them. I don't say that to excuse my behavior, or to attempt to lessen what was done to my son and daughters. I'm stating it as a fact of life: What I knew is what I dealt out. While I don't believe that it reached the level that I endured in my own childhood, what I did to my children was still very damaging.

I was wracked with suicidal depression and CPTSD (a complex form of post-traumatic stress disorder), sometimes in such overwhelming waves that I couldn't cope on even a rudimentary basis. I was cutting myself but feeling no pain, totally disconnected from myself. Finally, I had to turn my children over to Oklahoma Child Protective Services and lose my parental rights.

The youngest two were adopted, but, thank God, we are all still in touch.

One of my biggest regrets in regards to my children is that I didn't realize I needed healing. I had no idea of the pain I was feeling or the level of demons I was battling from my childhood. I knew something was wrong, I just didn't know what it was or how to fix it.

Sankofa—return and recover

I learned about Sankofa at the Marcus Garvey leadership charter school in Oklahoma City, where my children attended school for a while. At first, I didn't know how profound this term was or how this way of thinking would affect my life. Sankofa stands for a symbol used in Ghana, West Africa—a drawing of a bird with its head turned backward, taking an egg from its back, and holding it carefully in its beak. The symbol reflects the value of reaching back to past knowledge and bringing it into the present in order to make progress. Translated, Sankofa means, "Go back and get it."

On my journey to mental wealth, I learned I had to return to my past so that I could recover from my childhood trauma. I had no idea how profoundly those past wounds were affecting my present and my future. I had no clue how much my actions and my reactions stemmed from the challenges, abuses, and traumas I went through as a child. To this very day, I'm still pulling up pain from my childhood that affects the way I think and act.

I've found the most challenging part of Sankofa is that you must ask for help. In order to recover from the pain from the past, you must have assistance. After all, you did have quite a bit of help in creating the mental challenges, so it only makes sense that you have some help *un*creating them. Better yet, *uprooting* them feels closer to reality.

You can request many forms of assistance, and which type you choose is completely up to you. I discovered that finding the right type for me was a journey in itself, and I went through several forms of counseling and mental health therapy before finding the right remedies. Yes, my chosen path of recovery is multifaceted.

One of the facets of my mental health regime is natural medicine. I've always been a firm believer in herbal medicine. I especially chose this particular method of treatment after a very long and arduous journey through the world of prescription medication therapy. I had experienced many negative side effects, including many rashes, spasmed muscles, and chest pains. My most severe side effect was some slight heart damage. This is why herbal remedies are my choice of treatment.

Psychotherapy is another facet of treatment that I use to help control my mental health challenges. My therapist does a form of talk therapy referred to as psychoanalysis, the school of thought founded by Sigmund Freud. This form of talk therapy has worked tremendous wonders for me. I went from feeling very disconnected, suicidal, and difficult to reach, to being a person who is very aware of my mental thought processes and challenges, and actively mitigating them through mindfulness.

When I first started working with my therapist, I still experienced times when my first thought was escaping through suicide whenever the slightest issue arose. Now I am able to use the techniques my therapist has taught me to get to the base of the issue. During the last six years of psychotherapy, my mind has been gradually retrained to think of solutions rather than ways to escape, which had been my way of coping my entire life. My CPTSD (complex post-traumatic stress disorder) is somewhat unusual because I can't remember any time in my life *before* my trauma. Most people have a "before" and remembering that time is part of their treatment. I just don't have any "before."

I have worked with Dr. Cecile McKenna for my entire course of treatment, and I am incredibly grateful for the changes I have experienced. For three years, I was free of suicidal thinking of any kind, though a recent major life event, unfortunately, caused a small relapse. However, I realize I am still a work in progress, just like everyone else. I do not consider this a failure or a setback, it was just me being tested to see how serious I am about maintaining my mental health.

A service dog is the third facet of treatment that helps with my mental health challenges, giving me security and confidence every moment of the day or night. Ambassador joined me as a nine-month-old pit bull mix puppy on December 31, 2014. I chose to take on the task of adopting him and training him myself because of the extensive wait periods for psychiatric service dogs.

Training Ambassador proved to be more rewarding than I ever bargained for. The person I am today is a far cry from the person I was before getting Ambassador. I have learned to be patient, not only with the training process and teaching but also with learning—to have that same level of patience with myself. You see, Ambassador and I had to overcome language barriers in order to be able to communicate. I say that because as much as we'd like to think our dogs speak English (or German, or French, or Spanish), they don't.

Dogs can memorize a few words, but what they truly understand are our energies, gestures, and tone of voice—our nonverbal cues—which meant I had to learn to conduct myself differently. Honestly, I think I trained myself more than I trained the dog. In any case, Ambassador has been an incredible asset to my mental wealth. He knows the moment my mood starts shifting, and he's right there for me.

While my original intent was to just have a service dog, Ambassador has been far more than that. He has been a true partner in my success during the last five-and-a-half years.

I have many other tools in my mental wealth toolbox, but these three are the primary sources of maintaining my mental wellness.

It's your turn now

I'm passing the baton to you. It's time for you to assess where you've been, the challenges that you've overcome, and most of all, what your mental wealth is. What will you use in your wellness toolbox? Just simply reading this book, studying these chapters, absorbing these stories is not enough. It's time to get up and do the work.

I can't promise you a bed of roses or a bowl of cherries. The only thing I can guarantee is that the results will be worth the work. So when you're hit and you're hit hard, just remember these two lines from one of my favorite poems:

> *So stick to the fight when you're the hardest hit. It's when things seem worse that you must not quit.*
> **—*Don't Quit*, by John Greenleaf Whittier**

Eventually, you will reach a point when you know it's time to say to someone else . . .

*It's **your** turn now. What do **you** have?*

Author's Notes

My first memory is of being raped repeatedly when I was three years old. Since that time, I have overcome many challenges in my life.

The oldest of four children, I was born in Columbia, South Carolina. We moved often until we finally settled in Oklahoma, where I lived most of my life. As a young, single mother of three children, I had to give up custody of my children because of severe depression and complex post-traumatic stress disorder. Since that time, I have built a support system that is helping me achieve a level of mental wellness and wealth that I never thought possible.

A serial entrepreneur, I now live in Philadelphia with my service dog, Ambassador, a pit-mix rescue dog that is at my side night and day. I consider Ambassador to be my furry partner in success, both professionally and personally. With Ambassador at my side, I am determined to show others there is a way out.

I am training to become an inspirational speaker, and this is my first book.

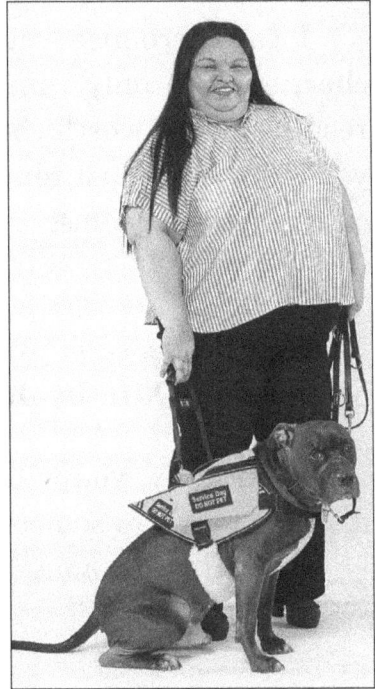

Contact info:

Email: buumbabe.bass@gmail.com
Facebook: Buumbabe Bass
Twitter: @buumbabe
Instagram: @buumbabe.bass
YouTube: Buumbabe & Bass

Chapter 16

Build Your Mental Wealth With Joy, Not Jealousy

Joe Peach Graves

D id you know that the hardest mountain to climb isn't the tallest? It isn't the steepest, the most jagged, or the most slippery. It has nothing to do with hazards or weather. The hardest mountain to climb is the one you didn't see coming until you slam into it. It's also the one you aren't equipped or prepared to climb.

Think of a time in your life when you had the rug pulled out from under you, and the last thing you wanted to hear was why you should look on the bright side.

When I stood 19,341 feet above Tanzania at the peak of Mt. Kilimanjaro, I had no idea that my greatest challenge was still waiting for me. A week later, after spending time on safari with one of my closest friends and mentors, I was on my way home from Africa and looked forward to seeing my wife and daughter. I was still exhilarated and thrilled by having climbed the world's largest free-standing mountain, something beyond the wildest dreams of most people. Ready to get on the plane, standing alone in the Addis Ababa Bole International airport, I read a Facebook message: Divorce papers were ready for me to sign and I should pick my daughter up from my wife's boyfriend's house once I landed.

> *You can reach a new level of mental strength and health when you don't waste your energy on jealousy, pain, and unhappiness.*

I felt gutted.

Right now you probably have questions, and the big one is *What's in this chapter to help me?*

Maybe you have experienced the pain of seeing a relationship come to an end. Maybe you learned that someone whom you love is in love with someone else. Maybe none of this relates to you, but you're just curious. What *I* know is this: the relationships we build reflect the most important aspects of our lives. If you want to grow your mental wealth in the realm of relationships, you might be able to learn a thing or two.

Just before I wrote this chapter, our family celebrated my daughter Jolinda's eighth birthday, which she happily said was the best day ever. Most people can't imagine how my family got where we are now from where we were the day I was walloped with an unexpected divorce. It may seem even more improbable to realize I work with families all over the world and help them learn a mindset of *compersion,* the first step on the path to living in Paradise Forever.

Love really does conquer all. Loving intentionally is how I survive and thrive after my rather traumatic forced change. I believe most people want to love unconditionally, and they do manage to do so until conditions occur that they're not prepared for. What brings me joy is helping people prepare mentally to love in *all* conditions, so they can focus on shining their light in the universe. I am passionate about this mission beyond all things, other than the love I have for my daughter.

Compersion is the opposite of jealousy. It's an ability that exists in all of us—the ability to feel joy in others' happiness. When I worked at Walt Disney World, I saw this emotion all the time. I witnessed a lot of it, performing with my friend Goofy, who I've known for years. Imagine the world before COVID-19, when after waiting in line for hours, a child finally has a turn to give Goofy the biggest hug ever.

The joy the child and his family feel is completely understandable. What I found even more amazing is the joy shared by people just walking past when they catch a glimpse of the child's ecstatic hug—they smile, melt a little, and share in the love. There is a strong possibility you at this very moment are smiling at the vision of a little kid getting blissed out with Goofy love.

Think about it. You're not feeling the joy and love because it's you or your child hugging Goofy. You're not

187

feeling jealous because the anonymous child got a hug from Goofy instead of your child (or you!).

The joy you feel is *compersion.* It's such a beautiful concept, but most people have never heard the word. In fact, your phone or computer will try to correct your spelling if you type it as a text or in a letter, but that is how it's spelled.

Compersion is not used widely because it's primarily associated with polyamorous relationships. Its definitions include the love and joy one feels for their partner when they are doing *much* more than just hugging Goofy.

At Disney, we shared a joke about Mickey Mouse going to relationship counseling with Minnie Mouse. Mickey shares why he is having a problem. The counselor says, surprised, "Mickey, be reasonable. You know Minnie is a cartoon character. Why are you so upset that she's a little silly?"

Mickey snaps, "I didn't say she was a little silly. I said she was f****ing Goofy."

The day I auditioned and earned a role as a Disney cast member, I heard this joke for the first time. Little did I know then that I would get married and have an ethically non-monogamous relationship with the mother of my child, a woman I love and respect to this day.

I know what you're thinking: *How can you believe in compersion if you lost your wife?*

But, you see, my divorce actually solidified my belief in compersion. I recognize how well this mindset has served me in our relationship, in business, and life as a whole, ever since I got the news when I was alone in Ethiopia.

Climbing Kilimanjaro and going on safari was part of the most epic vacation of my life. It was a vacation I earned partly through the joy I receive in helping others have joy. As a professional tourist, I work to help improve the quality of people's lives by showing them how wonderful vacationing feels and providing them with access to systems designed to save them money— and even make money—by living their best life.

The more people I help, the more money and opportunity for travel I earn. Because of this work and my genuine love for seeing the world, I've been to 43 countries and 38 states in the United States. I genuinely want to see the joy on my family's and friends' faces, so it came pretty easy to me and I excelled from the beginning.

Before I left on this vacation, I spent a few weeks visiting family in Colorado and California, before heading northwest to spend my birthday with my mother. She lives in a beautiful little house on the Oregon coast in a town that's so small, if I said its name, people would know the house. The two of us spent a couple of days alone, then my wife and daughter flew in from Honolulu to help me celebrate. We ate breakfast at the Pig & Pancake and had an amazing day playing in my mom's yard with her dog.

After Jolinda went to sleep, my wife and I went out for a night on the town. We shared what I still remember as one of the best days of my life. The next day my wife flew off to attend one of our company conventions, and

I went to Africa. I wasn't aware that was the last night we'd spend together as a married couple.

While I was in Africa, though my wife was surrounded by our team members and friends, she says she felt alone. For the last year, she'd been dating a guy off and on, and he didn't share our belief in compersion. She decided she didn't believe in it anymore either. After our ten years together, she was ready for a monogamous relationship. She picked up Jolinda at my mom's house, went back to Hawaii, and reconnected with the man who is now her husband.

I honestly believe he is a really great guy, and appreciate the amazing opportunities he has given my (now) ex-wife and daughter. Don't get it wrong. Despite my belief in compersion, divorce was not remotely fun; it is very painful. I was aware of him as her boyfriend the whole time, and I knew he loved her, yet I had absolutely *no* expectations our marriage would end. We had a life together, a child, a business, and I believe, a shared deep love. Now I was suddenly faced with crippling debt, custody issues, and the loss of a nearly 10-year partnership, in business as well as in marriage.

Again, I know what you're thinking: *You aren't really selling this whole compersion idea. It sounds terrible.*

Okay, I have a question for you: *What if I hadn't known about the guy at all?* Studies suggest one in three unmarried and one in five married relationships experience some form of infidelity. Think about it. You may have had an extramarital fling, or surely you know someone else who has been on one side or another of an affair.

190

One of the main differences in a compersion-based relationship is there's *honesty* between partners rather than lying.

Another big advantage of a compersion-based relationship is it's an amazing feeling when you are comfortable sharing everything with your partner. The freedom to speak about and act on the things you really want without guilt or judgment is more fulfilling than most will ever understand. The incredible sex, financial abundance, adventure, love, joy, passion (and did I say incredible sex?), that I've had through my belief in the power of compersion has been life-changing. I'll share more in my next book.

I don't plan to become polyamorous, so why even read this chapter, you wonder.

So, how *can* compersion help you? You don't need to change your monogamous lifestyle. Compersion is a philosophy that doesn't need to include any sexual extremes. It can simply be your conscious choice to reduce jealousy. It's a sign of mental strength.

I have an exercise for you. On a sheet of paper, draw a big plus sign, creating four quadrants on the page. On one line write *Joy* and on the line that crosses it write *Pain*. All the relationships you will ever have can be described on this sheet of paper. There will be moments in each quadrant in almost every relationship, but there will usually be a focus on one.

Schadenfreude. This German word describes the joy you feel when someone feels unhappiness, misfortune, or pain. (This is pronounced *shah*-duhn-*froy*-duh, and literally translates as *harm-joy*.) If you are in a relationship like this, your partner had better remember their safe word.

All jokes aside, very few people will admit to living in this quadrant, but they are out there. Actually, almost all of us feel schadenfreude sometimes. With our current political climate, regardless of what side you are on, there will be a lot of people who will feel joy when the other side loses. My mentor and co-author Johnny Wimbrey calls them *wolves*. They actually experience joy as they exercise their purpose to kill, steal, and destroy.

Jealousy. The next quadrant is for those of us who feel pain when someone feels joy—the *opposite* of compersion. Beyond feeling awful, living in this quadrant can create major problems. Have you ever had a friend snag a position or a customer that you wanted? How did it make you feel and did that feeling serve you?

Competition can be a motivator, but my belief is that friendly competition is better than a bitter rivalry. I teach my daughter to be a good winner and a better loser. When she doesn't win, she says with a smile, "Great job, I'm going to beat you next time!" This is a mantra in our family that helps us maintains drive without succumbing to jealousy.

Empathy. The third quadrant is when you feel pain at the pain of others. Too many people live in the empathy quadrant, simply because they don't want to live in the first two and they don't understand the last one. While being empathetic may seem like a good, generous quality, many don't take any action to find their way out of pain. They wallow in the pain and end up just attracting more pain. Remember, the first and best step to eradicating poverty is to not be in poverty yourself. In much the same way, the best way to eradicate sadness is to not be sad.

Compersion. If you really think about it, this is the square that everyone should want to live in. Right? It's where the party's at, but more importantly, it is where the mentally strong, mentally healthy folks live.

This concept is what helped me climb Kilimanjaro. When my business partner and former cruise director, Ray Carr, asked me to join him on this adventure, I had never even considered climbing any mountain. I worked with my father on his site, *AfricanJewelry.com*, so I knew I'd go to Africa someday, but hadn't thought of Tanzania. I owned no climbing gear, and because I live on Oahu, I can't stand the cold. I'm a wimp and firmly believe schools should close at anything below 60 degrees. The only reason I agreed to go is that I wanted to see Ray make it to the top, and I knew my being there would help him make the ascent. As I took step after step up that mountain, somehow freezing and sweating at the same time, my determination to get him to the top kept me going.

The ascent was thrilling, and I am glad for every moment of our trek. We camped at just over 15,000 feet the night before we reached the summit, and I saw an unforgettable, otherworldly scene that will inspire me for my whole life. We were above the clouds that night, and it was so cold that frost settled on top of the fluffy white clouds hugging the mountain below us. The stars

193

reflected off the frost, twinkling below me, and I felt as though I was drifting in outer space.

If I hadn't been focused on serving the joy of others, I never would have the opportunity to be there for that rare sight.

They say luck is what happens when preparation meets opportunity. Compersion is the mindset that prepared me for the greatest challenges and the greatest accomplishments in my life. I truly feel it has enriched my mind.

When Jolinda turned eight years old, she was surrounded by the love, support, and cooperation of both her parents, her stepfather, my partner and her son, one of my lovers along with her girlfriend and her girlfriend's boyfriend, who just happens to be my cousin and lives with us. It is the family we choose. I could have allowed jealousy to rob my daughter of that experience.

How much has jealousy cost you?

You can reach a new level of mental strength and health when you don't waste your energy on jealousy, pain, and unhappiness. I invite you to stop living in a quadrant of pain. Choose *joy*—live your life with compersion.

Author's Notes

As the great-great-grand-child of a runaway slave, I was raised in the spirit of generational improvement. I'm known both as a jack of all trades and a visionary leader, and my varied career paths and life experiences have given me some unique insights and the ability to connect with just about anyone. Being reared in Hawaii and having the pleasure of traveling to more than 40 countries and nearly every state has given me a perspective on paradise, plus the means to find happiness and freedom.

The majority of my entertainment career was spent with the Walt Disney Company, where an understanding of the Happiest Place on Earth expanded my mindset to the point that I learned anything is possible. When I was an assistant cruise director on the Norwegian Cruise Lines flagship, I gained an understanding of leading teams and exceeding expectations. My experience as an athlete and as a champion gamer honed my competitive nature. I also participate in slam poetry contests.

My experience as a father created my demand for a brighter future plus the patience and passion to teach. A combination of these and other life experiences gives

195

me the ability to inspire and educate learners to find solutions toward increase. With the belief that success is the progressive realization of a worthy ideal, I guide students on a path of self-discovery. Living in paradise forever is a reality every human can achieve, beginning right now.

I live in my own Hawaiian paradise, sharing custody of my daughter, Jolinda Peach Kamana'olana Graves, and increasing my love daily.

Contact Information:

Email:	joepeach@paradiseforeverhawaii.com
Facebook:	Joseph Peach Graves
Instagram:	@paradiseforeverhawaii

Chapter 17

Becoming

Savanna Lei

What are you becoming?

What's your attitude toward life? Is the glass half-empty or half-full?

There's one correct answer: The glass is both half-empty and half-full. What *you* say as you look at it depends completely on your perception.

Perception is everything! The way you perceive the outside world is the direct reflection of the way you perceive your inner being. The bad news is if you don't like who you've become, then it is difficult for you to see the beauty in the world. The good news is if you don't like who you've become, then you have the chance to become someone else.

This may sound impractical. I assure you, it's not. Think about it: *The starting point of all achievement is desire.* If you truly desire to become someone or something else, you must feed your desires every day. It makes absolute sense. To become a doctor or to join the ranks of most professions, you must dedicate extensive time and effort every day to become what you desire. Achievement doesn't happen overnight.

> **What's your true self and how do you want the world to see you?**

As a child you have no choice: You are given your name, you are taught the ways of your household, how to speak the language, and you are mentored by your family and community. You become the sum of your people, places, and things you know without the ability to choose any of them. But when you become an adult, you have the choice to choose whomever you'd like to be. You have the choice to re-brand yourself.

So, what will your rebirth look like? What's your true self and how do you want the world to see you?

Sometimes the regrets from our past keep us from becoming our true selves. If you're feeling regretful, take time to forgive yourself. You're only regretful because you learned your lesson, and you won't make the same choices if you have a do-over. Let's rename those regrets and instead call them character builders, lessons, or experiences.

We tend to be *so* hard on ourselves. Until the day we die, everyone on earth is trying to figure out this thing called *life*—and none of us has yet! Don't feel like you are alone with the bad decisions you have made. No one fails on their own, and no one succeeds on their own. Just don't place all the blame on yourself. People along the way helped you fail, and they will help you on your path of success, as well. We all play a role in someone else's life.

Too many people look for something they can take to fix them, some magic pill. There is no magic pill. The magic is within you; you are not broken. You are just the sum product of the people, places, and things you keep replaying in your brain and keep around you.

We hear people say, *Stop being negative. Stop looking in the past, get over it!* They just never bother to tell us how to stop. Let's face it, most of what we humans do is involuntary. Part of our problem is that we've never taken the time to unlearn all we'd learned as a child.

My secret recipe

As Ralph Emerson once said, *A man is what he thinks about all day long.* We all need to monitor our thoughts. The part of the brain that's responsible for emotions and memory is the same part that activates our fight-or-flight response. Negative or positive thoughts make our bodies react as though we're in an actual event. It's possible that negative thoughts make us sick, feel stressed, and even age us.

Is there a secret recipe to redirect your mind from negative thoughts? Indeed, there is, and I'd like to share it with you.

The secret is having *goals*—long-term goals plus short-term goals that pave the way to your long-term destination. There are seven different types of goals: *physical, financial, career, family, social, spiritual,* and *mental health* goals.

When you imagine and describe each one of these goals, it's important to be incredibly detailed because you want to get *exactly* what you ask for. The more detailed your goal is, the easier it is for you to consciously seek it. There is no limit to the movie you can create in your mind, so don't be stingy with your imagination when you build the descriptions. If you were in the market for an all-white brick farm home with dormers, black shutters, and a wrap-around porch with a swing, I am one-hundred-percent sure you wouldn't drive by a home with that description and not notice it.

Write your long-term goals down for each of the goal categories, and add an expiration date (that's when you'll update them). Use every detail when painting your mental images. When you write your financial goals, for instance, make sure you include in detail how you plan to earn this money and how you will pay it forward.

This is your movie. You're the producer, director, and screenwriter of your own movie. It's up to you to choose the characters you want in your life. It's up to you to write your story.

You must monitor the thoughts that you run throughout your mind and play on your mental movie screen. If you replay anxiety, negativity, and self-pity in your mind, projecting the frightening mental images over and over, it's equivalent to replaying a horror movie until you are numb to the violence. This is your creation, *only yours*—your design, your own horror movie—with a one-person audience. You. If you aren't careful with the thoughts that run throughout your mind, then the thoughts will run you.

Tragedies may affect you while you're in the process of becoming who you intend to be. That is why you work on your new identity every day—for that time when these unseen trials and tribulations come. Build yourself stronger, build that shield of armor into your screenplay, make yourself tough so you can take a harder hit without falling down. Life is no paradise, and you will be hit hard when you least expect it, but as you develop your physical, spiritual, financial, family, career, and mental health, you won't be so easy to knock over.

Keep the paper with your thoroughly-described goals in a place you can see easily. It's important that you start your morning and end your evening reading your goals *out loud,* which will trigger your cognitive recognition. Your morning recitation should be before you get on your phone or speak to anyone. Spend thirty minutes in deep thought; watch your mental movie, and see yourself in the role you will play in each individual goal.

Before bed, spend time visualizing what your life will be like when you reach your goals. Take the time to picture your new self in that movie, living your goals, and work toward being that person.

Just as an addict's mind knows when it's time for a fix, your mind will soon crave being able to focus on your goals and your new self every day. By spending time every day creating detailed new memories, you'll have a place in your mind to run to whenever a negative thought comes a-knocking.

Whenever a negative, insecure, and doubtful thought enters your mind, redirect it, and push it away within five seconds. Go to your goals and replay the movie of your detailed future.

When you apply my secret recipe, you must have faith, belief, and a burning desire. In the words of Mamie Brown's little boy, Les Brown, **You gotta be HUNGRY!**

202

The past isn't all it's cracked up to be

I was raised in the ghetto by a single mother of three children. My mother never drove a car, so we walked everywhere, rain, sleet, or snow. Even now, I thank my mother for my strong legs and agility. Our community had what I thought was the normal kind of life—poverty, drug addicts, drug dealers, prostitutes, people selling their food stamps, and thieves coming into homes trying to sell VCRs and other stolen goods (which we sometimes bought if the price was right).

Because my mom wasn't on drugs, I looked at myself as one of the lucky ones. As unsafe as my neighborhood was, it seemed to be the only place I truly felt safe. Most of the kids in my school had similar circumstances, and we all sure had poverty in common. Though I couldn't afford sports or any activities, I once played the flute for my school because it was free. I was damn good at playing that flute!

I often wondered if there was more to life than met the eye. It was the little things I saw that made me feel there might be more, like the child who came to school with a lunch box and snack pack. Or the child who came to school with all their school supplies and new clothes on the first day of school. They seemed like they had it all figured out. I often wondered why it was so different for me.

Our television only had two channels, and you could only watch it until they broadcast the Pledge of Allegiance. Out of boredom, I would watch The 700 Club or Matthew Lesko infomercials. I just knew there was more to life than what I saw in my neighborhood.

One Halloween, I went trick-or-treating into what I believed at the time was a rich area, though looking back now, it was probably barely middle class. I was blown away! I couldn't believe how clean the neighborhood was, how the homes were bright with fall and Halloween decorations, and how they smelled like fall-scented candles or a homecooked meal.

Suddenly, I didn't care about the candy; I just wanted to walk up the sidewalks and look into houses to see how clean and beautiful they were. I finally realized where all the kids with the lunchboxes and backpacks lived. After a long night of trick-or-treating, I didn't care at all about sorting through my pillowcase full of candy. I went to my room, stretched out on my bed, and thought of all the beautiful homes and great things I'd seen that night.

I no longer thought about what I didn't have, and I started to have a burning desire for what *I could have.* I realized it is not normal to be poor. I had decided I was going to be rich and move into a beautiful home and buy hundreds of fall-scented candles.

My mother told me we lived in poverty because I didn't have a father, which I found hard to believe. Even then, I believed deep inside that we could live in better conditions if she had just realized how beautiful and smart she was. As a child, it was more of a feeling, and I couldn't put it into words. I felt that even if we didn't have the nicest things, we would have a rich home if she would fill herself with love, faith, and self-confidence.

204

For weeks on end, I listened to *I Wanna Be Rich,* a song by R&B duo Calloway. R&B wasn't the usual choice of music in our all-Black and Hispanic community.

My dreams of being rich and buying a beautiful home with scented candles were soon ground away by poverty, sexual abuse, mental abuse, conditioning, conformity, and a visit to jail, which earned me a felony conviction. I had finally become one of *them.* I had finally conformed.

Life had kicked me down and I didn't know how to get back up. Les Brown once said, *If you fall, try to land on your back, because if you can look up, you can get up.* I wasn't on my back. I was face down with my head buried. Mr. Brown followed up that first saying with, *If your face is down, try to roll over because then you are one step closer to getting up.*

I didn't want to get up! I would have preferred to have just died. I didn't know much of anything, and what I did know, landed me in jail. Then, one day, I spontaneously became sick and tired of being sick and tired and changed my mind.

Most importantly, I started to change my attitude towards myself. I used to be so mad at God for my life. I stopped being angry with myself, with others, and with God, and I changed the way I spoke. Little by little, I began to work on myself. I was *becoming*. Through self-education and making better choices, I was able to see the value in myself.

Life had this strange way of just working out for me. Opportunities just seemed to start to present themselves to me. I developed new interests. I suddenly found myself around new people, places, and things. I studied books. I attended motivational speeches. I worked on my relationship with myself and with God. I was achieving my seven goals: physical, mental health, spiritual, social, career, family—all but financial.

205

Finding a purpose

But one key factor in this change process was still missing: I couldn't find my purpose. After all the self-care I pursued, I still couldn't find my purpose. I still couldn't find how to make a difference in the world.

To find my purpose, I spent a lot of time alone and in silent meditation, and finally, I realized what I *am* good at!

For my entire life, I've had that special touch that makes people feel better about themselves. Without any effort, I seem to see the worth in every individual. I can see people not only as they are, but what it took for them to get there. I can see the inner child in people, and I believe I have the ability to show people how important they are. I feel we all deserve to have someone to help us find and develop our greatness and purpose, and I believe that person is me.

My purpose is to lend a hand when someone is knocked down, lift them up, and love them; it just took me a while to discover it. Whatever you generously give in life will surely be returned to you with greater value. I feel worse for the people who don't give unto others, for they never receive the gift I receive when I give. The gratitude you get from giving to others is abundant. I should thank the less fortunate for the feeling I get when helping them.

This led me to start my nonprofit, StepUp Mentoring, a respite home community to help youth find their purpose while they have a safe place to live. I worked with a mastermind group to develop the nonprofit, and with a family court judge to design this alternative community for children ages 8 to 18 who'd otherwise be locked up or on the streets.

We're buying five acres of land, and the architect is drawing up plans for an expandable community of group homes. Each child will have a room, stable and well-trained house parents, and a safe long- or short-term place to live.

My focus expanded beyond helping children when I began taking care of Leonidus, a dog with cancer. He was 10 years old when he became sick and the vet gave him only 30 days to live. Leonidus and I developed an amazing connection, and I felt we truly communicated. I loved him so much that I would have done anything to keep him with me, so I cooked human-grade meals for him with anti-inflammatory herbs. I was able to keep him happy and healthy for more than a year until he died in my husband's arms on Father's Day, 2019.

I had been so happy taking care of him that I couldn't see myself not preparing these meals for other dogs. It was heart-breaking to see dog owners go through the same thing my family and I went through, and everyone agrees a dog's diet has a lot to do with its health. I decided to make a business out of the recipes I prepared for Leonidus and started K9 Food Prep, a human-grade dog food company.

207

My next step was to design the Doggie Café, which will be attached to my commercial kitchen. It's a lounge area where pets can try a buffet of gourmet treats, their human parents can try some bakery treats, and they can hang out together. The walls will be lined with freezers stocked with K9FoodPrep food. All plans for both businesses came to a halt due to the coronavirus, and we plan to relaunch in Spring 2021.

Yes, I used to want to be rich, but let's face it, everything we have goes to someone else when we pass away. The only thing you have that's *truly* yours is what you developed on the inside.

Self-worth, self-enterprise, wisdom, love, and understanding are the only things that can't be taken from us. Once you start understanding how important you are, you develop a different perception of the world. Make sure the path you are taking to your goals is building you into an amazing, loving person. Make sure what you are becoming will be filled with wisdom that you can pass on to others.

The real fulfillment comes from within, from when we are at work on ourselves. Always be thankful but never be satisfied. There is always more for you!

Author's Notes:

Over the years, I've found I definitely have an entre-preneurial spirit, and I look for-ward to being able to relaunch K9Food Prep and Doggie Café in 2021. I own two other successful and active businesses, Carbone Commer-cial Property, a billboard company, and Carbone Vacation Destinations.

Much of my energy is currently directed to the development of StepUp Mentoring; this nonprofit, with its respite community, is urgently needed. Innocent children are being locked up hours away from everything and everyone they know because there's no place for them in their own town.

I grew up in Utica, New York, with my single mother and two brothers, and have made my home in the same town with my husband and son.

Contact information

Email: K9foodprep@gmail.com
Website: K9foodprep.com
Facebook: K9FoodPrep
Instagram: @K9FoodPrep

Chapter 18

Program Your Mind for Success

Captain Rex Witkamp

I believe we all have our purpose in life. I believe we have greatness within each of us. Tragically, few find their greatness and live it. Those who don't find it carry around a heavy burden in their lives. Cartoonist Charles Shulz said, "There is no heavier burden than an unfulfilled potential." Imagine lightening your load just by living your passion.

I focus my life on motivating people to find and live their purpose. Living life by design and with purpose is not a new idea. It has been overlooked because it forces us to question our comfort zone. Ninety-seven percent of people live in their comfort zone. Three percent of people live in their effective zone. The difference between the two is growth, and growth is uncomfortable.

I can teach you how to beat the mediocrity mindset and rise to a new standard while visualizing the best version of your existence by living your purpose. It's easier to be yourself meaningfully than to wander through life wondering what you will be. Stop attempting to be—just be.

Imagine you are in a cancer support group meeting. Witness an empty room dulled by drab furniture and dust visible in the sunlight angling down from the windows. An older veteran who was recently diagnosed sits in the circle of chairs. He is alone in life, no family, no friends, no one to share his pain. He is depressed, anxious, stressed about his future, and clearly struggling.

> *Design the life you want to live. Living your dreams starts by envisioning yourself in that dream.*

212

Now, in walks a man who forgets about the failures of his past and the current challenges of his own diagnosis and starts to focus the conversation on the possibilities of the future. The new arrival shuts away his own reasons for giving up and empowers the older man with ideas of optimism, the search for meaning, the healing and influential power of his potential, and most of all, the importance and power of positive thinking.

The old man is transformed. He sits up in his chair and stops staring at the floor. His chest expands as he radiates a new level of energy. His voice gets louder, and his eyes light up with hope. He even smiles and starts to talk confidently about the possibilities of what he will do in the near future when he gets better.

I share this experience firsthand because I am the man who decided to use my voice for good, to use it to motivate and inspire someone else in his time of need. I benefited, too, and I walked out of the meeting feeling different, stronger, and with a healing of my own. I felt a sense of relief and reward I had never felt before. It felt natural to use something already in me to fulfill my purpose.

In that moment, I understood the difference between just being a part of something, and something being a part of you. It turns out it wasn't the diagnosis of a life-threatening illness that changed me: It was me living my purpose to deliver messages of encouragement, motivation, and strength through the power of my voice to help others so they would find their strength.

My purpose in life was revealed to me. That was my moment—the sense of relief came from finding my purpose and living my making instead of just making a living.

We all have seeds of greatness endowed to us by our Creator. We are made in His image, armed with a mission to fulfill the potential that is already ours. Here is my simple equation for greatness: You + God + Nothing Else = Greatness.

Because we are made in the image of God (Genesis 1:26), we have everything we need from the moment we were born.

Mark Twain said the two most important days of your life are the day you are born and the day you find out why. Expressed another way, Howard Thurman, one of Dr. Martin Luther King's mentors, said, "Don't ask what is the reason for life, ask what is the reason for your life."

We must shift our thinking back to being better students of ourselves. Thomas Lounsbury, an American literary historian, and critic, noted "We must view with profound respect the infinite capacity of the human mind to resist the introduction of useful knowledge."

Eric Hoffer, a moral and social philosopher of the 20th century, observed that "In times of change, learners will inherit the earth, while the learned find themselves beautifully equipped to deal with a world that no longer exists.

It is our duty to learn as though we will live forever and teach as though we will die tomorrow. We are never too old to learn, and never too young to teach.

We must be willing to program our minds for success. We all want results in our lives, yet few establish the connection between programming and results: programming creates beliefs, beliefs create attitudes, attitudes create feelings, feelings determine actions, and actions create RESULTS. If you want results in your life, start by programming your mind for success!

The world deserves to know what you have to offer. Everyone has greatness, and this is something you already know! Commit to making the change you need to succeed in order to win at life! It's time for you to rise up and be a 24-hour champion!

If you do the things in life that are easy, life will be hard. If you do the hard things, your life will be easy!

214

It will be your perception and attitude of the overall situation that steers you to the better outcomes in life.

Consider these two quotes about attitude:

Captain Jack Sparrow (*Pirates of the Caribbean*) said, "The problem is not the problem. Your attitude about the problem is the problem."

Charles Swindoll said, "Attitude is more important than facts. It is more important than the past, than education, money, circumstances, than failures and success, than what other people think, say, or do. It is more important than appearance, ability, or skill. It will make or break a business, a home, a friendship, an organization."

Life has challenges of all kinds: sickness, disease, deaths, loss of income, loss of business, loss of property; the list of losses goes on and on and on.

But the bright side for all of recorded history is that the storylines for struggle and achievement always repeat. There will be no testimony without a test first, no gain without pain. It's not what happens to you, it only matters what happens in you.

Your important assignment in your life is to carry out your purpose. A person convinced against his will is of the same opinion still. You must find your will. Where is your will, your moment to pursue your passion and fulfill your potential?

It is incredibly important, especially now, that we focus on our lives and our dreams and admit we are able to live our purpose with guidance from what I call my *Five Tenets*:

- Rise above mediocrity
- Elevate your standards
- Visualize the best version of yourself
- Live up to your highest potential
- Give purpose for your potential

And, because all of us have this brief moment in time to put our greatness to work for us, I think about those who believe they are not capable for whatever reason. The great American motivational speaker, Denis Waitley, shared this: "It's not what you are that holds you back, it's what you think you are not."

All of us were born for greatness, but only some of us will admit it. The largest odds are in our favor because we are already here!

Bahamian evangelist and author, Dr. Myles Munroe, explained from another angle: "The richest place on earth is not found in the oil fields of the Middle East, or the diamond mines of Africa . . . it is found in the graveyards of the world, that is where important books were never written, great ideas were never shared, awesome stories were never told, amazing experiences were never built on, future dreams were never acted upon, incredible inventions were never patented and given to benefit all of the rest of humanity."

What important assignments are you neglecting to accomplish toward your goals in life?

Here is another massive point to consider when programming your mind for success: You must work on yourself continuously.

Write down your goals and recite them out loud three times a day: morning, noon, and night.

216

Our lives are full of challenges and obstacles, and life owes you nothing! So, who else is going to work on your goals? Who else is going to work on your dream? Who else is going to act on your invention, your gift, your talent? If you don't do so on your own behalf, I guarantee you: someone else will for theirs!

When you grasp the importance of self-development, you will begin to notice changes in your surrounding circles of friends, acquaintances, business partners, and mentors. If you don't have a mentor, seek one out and learn as much as you can from them. Be open-minded with an open playbook, willing to learn at every level of life. Once I became a student of life, my life's challenges were more easily overcome. It will bring you higher highs, and higher lows, too.

Once I began to work on myself through self-development reading, going to lectures, listening to audiobooks and programs, seeking mentors, and being a mentor to others—everything changed!

The key is to work harder on yourself than you do at your job. If you provide more value than you are being paid, soon you will be paid for more than you are worth.

Consider the importance of never giving up, as illustrated by the story of a gold miner who went out west looking for gold. He found a likely mountain, at great expense bought the mining equipment he needed, and he worked his claim day after day. Weeks and years went by without finding the gold he was sure he would find in the mountain. The miner finally gave up his search and sold his expensive mining equipment for pennies on the dollar to a blacksmith who had no experience mining, but who realized there must be great value in the equipment. The miner moved back east and went back to selling insurance.

The blacksmith found the exact spot where the miner had quit, and he decided to mine in the same spot. After drilling and digging for no more than three feet, he struck a gigantic vein of gold in the mountain. Only three feet!

How many times do we quit when we might be only three feet from our gold? The next time you feel like giving up, remember this.

As you program your mind for success, you must be willing to serve others' needs in order to fulfill your own. What you volunteer and give back to those in need will be sent forth to the universe, multiplied, and returned to you. The Universal Law of Attraction is about helping others get what they want in life; and you will not have to worry about getting what you want out of life.

I want to talk a minute about your dreams of destiny. Where does destiny come from? Is it set in stone? Do people have the ability to change their destiny for the better?

When we talk about lives being programmed, we mean they're programmed either by default or by design. Unfortunately, most people live under the auspices of default. The few who are destined for greatness live their lives by design. All people are capable of designing their surrounding environments of body, self, spirituality, nature, physical, financial, network, and their relationships.

How?

- **Body**: by working out
- **Self**: growing your self-development and achieving your mastery of self
- **Spirituality**: cultivating your spirit
- **Nature**: improving the environment around you
- **Physical**: improving your physical living conditions
- **Financial**: increasing your financial net worth
- **Network**: improving your network of people and associations
- **Relationships**: by continually improving your relationships with other people.

By making better choices, you can design the environment of your life. You can change your environment, you can influence your environment, or you can leave your environment. Simply add, subtract, or shift the environments surrounding your life.

Can someone else determine your destiny? They can, but only if you let them by default. Design the life you want to live. Living your dreams starts by envisioning yourself in that dream. Make yourself the hero of your story, for that matter!

Dr. A.P.J. Abdul Kalam was one of India's most distinguished scientists and also served as the president of India. He said, "(A) dream is not that which you see while sleeping; it is something that does not let you sleep."

Leaders are comfortable with being uncomfortable. They know how to take calculated and decisive action with a time-sensitive matter. When timing is everything with an opportunity, they pounce! Opportunities to better themselves, opportunities to better others, opportunities to better their company, the economy, opportunities to better their community, and to change the world. To truly be rich means that you have found the ability to help elevate others' lives in your lifetime. Be a leader. Start with yourself.

I don't know about you, but I want to live a life of fulfillment and meaning. I want to lead a life of significance and purpose. An enriched life begins by staying busy doing the things that matter, rather than just counting the things you do to stay busy. Don't fool yourself by counting the things you do. Instead, get busy doing the things that count. Don't worry if others don't see your vision.

Digital Media Innovator and e-Commerce Pioneer, Jay Sammit, said, "It's better to walk alone than follow a crowd going in the wrong direction." You must begin to see this for yourself.

Galileo was quoted as saying, "You cannot teach a man anything; you can only help him find it within himself."

Belief does not come from success. Success comes from belief, and belief comes from the relentless pursuit of your potential.

Theodore Roosevelt said, "Far better is it to dare mighty things to win glorious triumphs even though checkered by failure, than to take rank with those poor spirits who neither enjoy much nor suffer much, because they live in the gray twilight that knows neither victory nor defeat."

The philosopher Nietzsche said, "If you know your why in life, you can endure almost any how." Your passion is your potential. Your potential is your purpose. Your purpose is your why.

In order to follow your passions in life, you must be willing to take risks.

But, Rex, will it be hard? Yes.

But, Rex, will I face challenges? Yes.

Will I get hurt? Yes.

Will it be worth it? Yes!

Life is not about what you do, it is about what you become. Ask yourself, *What am I becoming in life, in my job, my career, my relationships?*

All dreams will be tested for authenticity.

Be prepared to stare directly at the risks of following your passions and do them anyway. Do you want results? Start by programming your mind for success by living your life by design, not by default.

I challenge you to live my *Five Tenets*. They are so important to your future that I'm listing them again, and this time I'm including an extra level of guidance:

- *Always* rise above mediocrity
- *Continue* to elevate your standards
- *Purposefully* visualize the best version of yourself
- *Aggressively* live up to your highest potential
- *Meaningfully* give purpose for your potential

Now go forth with power and conviction to reach for and achieve what you deserve out of life: ***Program your mind for success.***

Author's Note

During the past 35 years, I've worked in at least 10 very different industries, in jobs ranging from busboy to U.S. Coast Guard-licensed boat captain, a paperboy to a paramedic, freelancer to firefighter. I can relate to most people's struggles with work, family, school, and finances. I've had great success in life building a big business, and I have hit rock bottom, been flat broke, behind on my bills and my dreams, kicked in the teeth by life, and almost killed off by cancer.

I'm also a best-selling author and motivational speaker who inspires everyday people to fulfill their potential in life by aligning their passion to achieve their purpose.

Contact Information

Email:	support@rexwitkamp.com
Facebook:	Rex Witkamp
Instagram:	@capt.rexwitkamp
Website:	www.RexWitkamp.com
Podcast:	Ready, Set, Live! Purpose Driven Potential

222

Chapter 19

Lessons From My Father
Trials will make you stronger

Linda Nefertiti

If you are going through hell . . . don't stop!
—Johnny Wimbrey

My earliest memory is still painful after all these years. When my elementary school teacher molested me in a darkened classroom, he changed my life. My teacher was an authority figure I had been taught to trust, and he violated that trust when he violated my young body and mind.

After I told my mother, she went to the school to confront him, a white man, and he denied my story, saying, "There's no way I would have touched a little nigger girl!" The principal backed him up, and they both said I was a troublemaker. By the time my mother left the office, she was repeating everything they had drilled into her head. I was doubly violated; the one person who was supposed to protect me let me down, too. I was left to fend for myself. In addition to losing my innocence, I lost my ability to trust authority, which led me to a myriad of problems.

As I built layers and layers of walls around myself and tried to keep people from getting close to me, I lost my trust in everyone. By the time I graduated from high school, I had been raped and abused again. My boyfriend tried to kill me while I was pregnant, and then I tried to end my own life.

> "
> *Sometimes the smallest things can have the greatest impact on life*

Fortunately, God had plans for me and my unborn child, and my firstborn son Akiiki was born in April 1973.

In the 1970s, I became good friends with my husband-to-be, and I knew immediately we were meant to marry. He had a daughter just six months older than my son and we had a rough time blending our families at first, but thank God we did. We moved to Houston and were married in 1979. Two years later, we had a son (Hodari) together and became one big, happy family.

When the children spent the summer of 1987 in Michigan with their grandparents, there were complications on the return trip. I ended up having to fly to Detroit to pick up my five-year-old son, whose ticket had been misplaced by the airline. Heading back, Continental Airlines had problems with our plane and rerouted Houston passengers onto Northwest Airlines Flight 255. I hated to fly in the first place, and after almost 13 hours at the airport, I was tired, frustrated, and refused to get on that plane with my son.

The other Houston-bound passengers boarded, took off—and moments later, we heard the plane crash and break apart. All passengers were killed except a four-year-old girl. I was terrified because I still didn't realize all the miracles God had already worked in my life.

Dig Deeper

In 2003, my husband was diagnosed with multiple myeloma, a rare and deadly cancer, and given only 11 months to live. During the seven years he survived, he always tried to make a difference in the lives of others. The day before my 56th birthday, he took his last breath. He fought a good fight and will forever be loved and remembered.

After he died in 2010, I started attending a neighborhood church, and even though I was not a member, I was asked to lead a small group. I agreed. For our study book, I chose *Dig Deeper,* by Nigel Beynon and Andrew Sach, not only to understand God's word better but to dig deeper into who I was. I had to uncover wounds that had been buried deep inside of me and had festered in my soul for decades.

I went about my daily life as if nothing was wrong; my lifelong tendency to hide pain gave me the ability to project strength. My sons knew I was suffering, but they were the only ones. At night I would lie across my bed and cry myself to sleep.

As I watched Oprah's show one night in 2011, Tyler Perry was talking about Oprah giving Morehouse College scholarships to 300 young African-American men. These young men were becoming doctors, lawyers, business owners—men of substance—thanks to Oprah paving the way.

I sat straight up in bed and told God I wanted to do something of that magnitude. I prayed and asked him to send me a vehicle that would help me financially and would allow me to make a difference in the lives of hundreds of others. A few days later, a friend of mine invited me to see a presentation and meet a couple who would change my life forever. They are still in my life and making a difference today, and I thank God for Edwin and Andrea Haynes.

Goal-Getting Sisters

Every Queen needs a tribe.
—Earlene Buggs

I formed a bond with a Mastermind group of women called Goal Getters and joined the group. As women with similar experiences, we set goals in the areas of business, finances, relationships, health, and spirituality.

One of my goals was to lead another small group, hoping it would bring me on a closer path to God. For our study book, I chose *Undaunted,* a book on human trafficking, written by Christine Caine. As I led the group, I decided to share my story. I was amazed at how quickly they all opened up and shared experiences they had never told anyone else! The book helped us strengthen our relationship with God. I was excited to learn several of them in turn became small group leaders and were also able to make a difference.

Visualize it, believe it, and you will have it

In life you don't get what you
want, you get what you picture.
—Holton Buggs

Best-selling author! dominates the center of one of the many vision boards hung throughout my condo. I've followed Johnny Wimbrey over the years; when we met in December 2019, we took a picture together, and I posted it on Facebook. Amazingly, today I'm co-authoring a book with Johnny, who's a best-selling author several times over. I used to fear flying, and now I feature the word *Travel* at the top of the same vision board. Since then, I've traveled to several international destinations and am part of a technology company that offers travel as its first vertical.

Early this year, I woke up one morning at 3 a.m. and found my vision board had fallen off the wall. When I picked it up, I was surprised at what I saw; in fact, I don't remember putting it on the board. But when I saw these words, I knew God was telling me what my purpose was: "It's been 10 years and 100 women making a beautiful difference in 1000s of lives."

The words made sense to me. My husband had died ten years before. In my first book, I wrote, "My purpose is to help 100 families earn a seven-figure income and change the financial fabric of their lives, while we enrich the lives of thousands around the world." Now I realized I could do this by helping 100 women.

Though it made sense, it shocked me because I'd never wanted to be a part of a big group of women. I now understand I am supposed to lead and guide 100 women . . . it must be part of God's divine order because that is clearly not something I would ever endeavor to do on my own.

I was once a member of a woman's group called Nzinga, in the Shrine of the Black Madonna. I recently reconnected with Gail Carr (Bayo), the group leader, and my former mentor, and she gave me a picture showing me standing in front of the group, as though I was leading. I have no idea when this picture was taken, but it was prophetic. Gail, who was once my mentor, has joined the technology business team that I lead.

Isolation can bring about inspiration

You are whole and complete no matter
what anyone else thinks of you.
—Lisa Nichols

After my husband's death, I found out for the first time what it was like to live alone. My condo is just 800 square feet, just the right amount of open space for me—a person with claustrophobia—to feel comfortable in. I was blessed to have the condo, for after his death I lost everything except my mind, and sometimes that was questionable. Moving into this condo helped me rebuild my life and my credit. I rode the bus and rented cars until I was able to afford a new vehicle. God gave me back everything I lost a hundred-fold, and now I'm driving a vehicle I have wanted for years, an Audi.

Living alone, awakened my creativity, and writing this poem was one of the results:

Queendom

We're encouragers and nurturers, among other things,
Goal-getting sisters, you know what I mean,
Nifty fifty, below and above,
A shoulder to lean on, we'll give you much love.
But don't get it twisted, our families we'll defend,
We're determined and on purpose, on us, you can depend.
We'll bend, but our motto is, you'll never get the best of me.
Instinct plus purpose together leads to destiny.
Goal-getting sisters, go build your Queendom, girls!
Change yourself first, then go change the world!

229

Last March, I left the office, took an empty elevator—and it suddenly stopped on the sixth floor. I pushed the alarm and tried to open the door. The inside door opened all the way, but the outside door opened just enough to let some air in.

Remember, I'm claustrophobic. Trying not to panic, I yelled and screamed, and three people came to my rescue. They couldn't get me out, and then the maintenance man discovered the elevator cable had broken. He told me how to turn the power off so that the elevator would not move again. Then he explained I was blessed that the elevator stopped on the sixth floor rather than plunging to the bottom floor.

It was clear I was about to be stuck in the elevator for hours and I had to make a decision. If I panicked like I normally do in a claustrophobic situation, I could have sent my blood pressure up, gone into convulsions, had a stroke—or worse, had a heart attack. I took deep breaths and called my accountability partner, Belivian Carter. She helped me create the condition in my mind that allowed me to visualize myself on the other side of the elevator door.

Then I called my prayer partner, Sundra Woodfolk (Adero); she prayed for me and continued to tell me to trust God. I sat down on the floor and stayed calm—and then the firemen showed up and turned out all the lights! Then they had to close the door! I thank God that I was able to keep my composure. I made it through my time in the elevator without incident.

Change is constant; my life experiences have helped me through some extremely rough times, but all glory belongs to God for the things he has brought me through! I have been constantly improving because of the books I read, the things I listen to, and the associations I have.

Recently I attended *Rise up Challenge,* a power-packed virtual summit put together by Pete Vargas, where 60 different world influencers spoke and poured wisdom into all of the participants. I'm extremely grateful to all the speakers in that summit for sharing their knowledge. One of those speakers was the motivational speaker and best-selling author, Les Brown. Now I am not only collaborating with Mr. Brown on this book, I am also part of his Power Voice speaker group.

In 2017, I made a conscious decision to be transparent and allow others to look at the adversities I'd experienced that still held me back. My chapter in *Positive Mental Attitude* included very personal testimonies, and once I shared them, I thought I could look forward to a brand-new life where I never needed to mention those terrible experiences again. I said I was an overcomer, and I expected everything to come up smelling like roses!

The problem was, I never dealt with the root of the problems, not until I wrote this chapter in *The Power of Mental Wealth*.

Though I had exposed my demons, I had not let them go. I've always been an encourager for other people, but there was a flip side to my positivity. I was strong because of the anger pinned up inside of me, because of my past hurts.

For the last several years, I have worked to make a difference. I continue to ask God to use me in a mighty way to show that he uses imperfect people for his Glory. I know he isn't through with me yet!

I have mentored young girls who are leaving middle school, heading into high school, and I am able to speak and share my story. This has helped some girls to open up to me about their experiences. It is fulfilling to be able to let them know they can make a difference and can be anything they put their minds to. I have also worked with women to make a difference in their lives, by sharing some of my story and my vision to help women.

Now I feel I am strong because I know who I am, *whose* I am, and what my purpose is. For the first time, I can see the root of the problem. In a recent conversation with my coach, he said these words and they stuck with me, "*Stop trying to do God's job!*"

At first, the words took me aback and gave me pause, but then I realized what he was saying. I always wanted to control whatever took place in my life. I believe everything happens for a reason and things do not manifest in our time. God is always in control!

My father taught me survival skills

Behind every challenge lies opportunity.
If you lament too long over
the challenge you will miss the opportunity.
—Edwin Haynes

On May 28, 2020, my 91-year-old father succumbed to cancer. He had served in the Korean War in the Army's 82nd Airborne Division as a paratrooper. He did two tough tours of duty between 1946 and 1954, and after serving his country, he moved us to Detroit, Michigan where he opened up Roger's Barber Shop. My dad employed many people from the community, again giving service.

When he died, racial tension was as bad as during the Detroit riots of 1967, when police lined the streets and we had to stay in the house because the community was filled with violence. It felt like déjà vu.

During the pandemic, we couldn't visit him because he was quarantined. My father let my other sisters know he was ready to transition; however, my youngest sister and I did not get to see our father before he made his transition. He tried to hold on until we arrived, however, when they told him our planes had landed safely he took his last breath. We were able to witness him being honored on a flag-covered bed, with the Veteran's Walk of Honor. Hearing the words, "Honored veteran leaving the floor," filled me with pride. He was my first mentor and hero and introduced me to the network marketing industry. Shortly after my father passed away, I learned some things about him I hadn't known, which taught me some things about myself as well.

With my father's death, my life was once again turned upside down. His death was not one of sadness, though; I drew strength from writing his obituary, and I knew I had to continue the legacy both he and my late husband left.

The realities of what happened with my father and the world-wide virus made me snap back to it. In all, I lost five family members and four friends within four months. On the other hand, I was blessed to gain Charity, my 28-year-old granddaughter whom I'd never met before but am now getting to know. I thank God that He gave me a strong constitution, a high tolerance for pain, and the power of mental wealth to push through and complete the journey that is set before me.

233

Author's Notes

As the third-oldest daughter of nine children born to Roosevelt and Mablene Rogers, family has always been important to me. I am grateful to still have my mother with me at the age of 89; she taught me how to persevere and maintain a strong faith in God.

My family also consists of my sons Akiiki (my rock), and Hodari (my music); a stepdaughter, Tishauna; two granddaughters, Charity and Akila; three grandsons, Jayden, JayVaughn, and Jaymarri; and a great-grandson, Ayden, who stole my heart. I love to sing, dance, make others laugh, travel, and write poetry. Tai chi and yoga also help me relax.

Though my formal education ended at high school graduation, I have gained a wealth of knowledge and a thirst to continue learning. I continue to participate in the network marketing industry because it offers personal self-development with a compensation plan attached and affords everyone an equal opportunity to succeed. For 35 years, I've worked in the financial and insurance industry, and I realize I enjoy it because of the service we render to others.

I dedicate my chapter in this book to the memory of my father, Reverend Roosevelt Rogers, Jr., and my late husband of 35 years, Robert (Hodari) Patton.

Contact information:

Email:	Lpatton11@hotmail.com
Facebook:	Linda Nefertiti Patton
Instagram:	@lnefpatton
Twitter:	@Lpattons11
LinkedIn:	Linda Patton

Chapter 20

Life's Ride: My Journey to the Paralympics

Deborah McAlexander

Life is like a horse show, an up-and-down ride.
Sometimes you fall, sometimes you glide.
Victory's about conquering adversity,
    one challenge at a time,
Guiding each step in God's rhythm and rhyme.
                    —Jack McAlexander, 1940-2017

During the 2019 Region 9 Dressage Champion-ships in Katy, Texas, I was walking to an outdoor arena when a man shouted, "Hey, blind lady, I can't believe it! You're walking in a straight line and you don't even have a guide dog." As I turned to face him, he pointed to my white cane. "Is that thing real? You don't look blind."

This wasn't the first time someone said that. I gave him my usual comeback, "What does blind look like?"

"Not like you! The blind people I know are pretty helpless."

I smiled. "Seeing with physical eyes can be deceiving. When you look at me, do you perceive that I am totally blind in my left eye and see through a tiny straw of central vision in my right eye?"

> **All things are possible when one rides by faith, not by sight!**

"Nope, you don't look, act, or talk like any blind person I've ever seen."

238 Pulling a paper straw from my pocket, I continued, "To help you experience how *I* see, please hold this straw in your right hand and position your fist against your right-eye socket. Cover your left eye with the palm of your left hand. No peeking! Since the age of 24, this has been how I see."

"Aha! You're not blind! You're cheating!"

I laughed. "You're not the first person to find my blindness confusing. Now that you understand how I see, can you imagine what it is like for me, a blind para-dressage* equestrian, to try to control a powerful, unpredictable horse with a mind of its own?"

Climbing the highest peaks in the Blindness Mountain Range has taught me that all things are possible when I ride by faith. I invite you to meet my dressage partner, Cornet Noir and watch us ride. We

will show you that losing eyesight is far less significant than losing *vision beyond eyesight.*

Are you looking for ways to conquer adversity and guide a victorious Life's Ride through the obstacles and failures blinding your pathway to happiness and success? Great! Cornet Noir and I bring you hope and help.

The dangerous nature of horse show competition and training parallels the uncontrollable environments people deal with daily. In the dressage arena, as well as in life, there is no guarantee of winning. Adversity is part of life, and learning to identify and solve problems is one of the biggest challenges we face.

Am I trying to discourage you? No! Victory is defined not only by the color of the medal or ribbon, or the status one reaches in society, but also by the obstacles and failures, we conquer on the way.

When you're bucked off during life's ride, you need to decide: Will you allow yourself to sit on your pity pot, or do you choose to find the mental toughness to get

239

Dressage is a high-level equestrian sport that evolved from calvary exercises; it has been an Olympic sport since 1912. The horse makes precise movements in a predetermined pattern, responding to its rider's almost invisible leg and body movements. Para-dressage is dressage for riders with an eligible permanent physical impairment as defined by the international organization, Fédération Equestre International (FEI), and it's the only equestrian sport in the Paralympics.

up, climb back on, and finish a triumphant ride on the horse that life has given you?

My journey through blindness

On Wings of Prayer, I journey through this life,
Lifted high, above all strife.
Yes, the darkness scares me, problems block my path,
Onward, upward, I will climb.
Trust in God, walk every step in faith,
Dare to dream a Mt. Paralympics dream.
Nothing is impossible, believe, work hard to win,
Never quit, reach for the stars.

—Deborah McAlexander

Because adversity happens to everyone, my story of overcoming trials and suffering cuts through every boundary between you and me. Being abandoned at birth by my biological mother and my adoptive parents divorcing dispelled any illusions of a fairy-tale life.

When I was twenty-four, blindness unexpectedly attacked the epicenter of my being. At that time, I was studying violin at the St. Louis Conservatory of Music. The ophthalmologist's blunt diagnosis, "You have retinitis pigmentosa and will be totally blind and deaf by the age of thirty," plummeted my life into a downward tailspin of terror.

Every morning I woke up wondering if I would see or hear anything at all. My dream of becoming a professional violinist was shattered. My positive, energetic spirit was broken. I felt like I had been bucked off my horse and trampled by a herd of wild horses. For several years, I wandered through life without direction, and you bet, I did a splendid job of sitting on my pity pot! Later, I learned that I'd been misdiagnosed. Yes, I was going to become almost completely blind, but I didn't have retinitis pigmentosa, and I didn't become deaf.

Meanwhile, my wandering took me to southern California, where I met my future husband. After Jack and I married and moved back to my hometown of Jefferson City, Missouri, Rehabilitation Services for the Blind (RSB) provided training for me at Program for the Blind in Kansas City, Missouri. I had always thought blindness was something that occurred during old age, or to a child who was born blind. At the school, I met individuals of all ages and from all walks of life who became blind for a variety of reasons. Did you know there are 21 million blind and visually impaired Americans? You see us every day, and in many cases, you don't recognize our invisible disability.

After completing my training, I earned a Bachelor of Music and Master of Music degrees in piano performance. I was unprepared for the obstacles I encountered with Missouri RSB when I developed a business plan to establish an independent piano studio and begin a motivational speaking career. During a small business review committee meeting with RSB and Missouri Protection and Advocacy staff, the RSB Deputy Director said, "Our position is to set the bar low; therefore, any gain is a success. You, Deborah, set the bar too high."

Two choices were before me: (1) compromise my high-bar standards and allow myself to be imprisoned in a "low-bar" blind box or (2) jump out of the box and

241

challenge the system. I chose to jump and challenge because losing eyesight is far less significant than losing *vision beyond eyesight.* I believe it's better to set the bar high and miss it than to set the bar low and always reach it.

Blindness does not define who I am. Blindness does reveal who I am.

During 30 years of personal happiness and success as a professional pianist and nationally recognized music educator, I continued to struggle with issues of self-concept. Despite years of psychological counseling, I often fell victim to the stereotypes surrounding blindness. I did not belong in the sighted world. I did not belong in the blind world. Although the physical loss of sight creates many challenges for me, my invisible disability is difficult for others to recognize when I'm not using my white cane. Because I don't fit the general public's expectations of what a blind woman should be, I've had to constantly defend my status as a person with a severe disability.

Jack and I were married for 30 years, 5 months, 21 days, and 23 3/4 hours. During the last 15 years of his life, Jack battled Parkinson's disease and Lewy Body dementia. On November 6, 2017, at 11:45 pm, he awoke from a coma, looked into my eyes, said, "Hi, Deborah, I love you," drew his last breath, and stepped into eternal life. In that instant, I knew I would again be challenged to redirect the focus of my life. This time, however, the focus would not be about me, but about how God could use me to glorify His holy name through an incredible journey guided by faith, not by sight.

242

The next summer, I found an exciting new direction for my life. During a trail ride, another horseback rider asked me if I had ever considered riding in the Paralympics. "The Parawhatics?" I asked, "Never heard of them." With my curiosity aroused, I began researching the Paralympic Games' only equestrian sport—para-dressage.

By the fall of 2018, I received National Classification for para-dressage competition based on my eligible permanent physical impairment. I learned I was the only U.S. rider with visual impermanent in any of the five grades at that time.

I am an experienced saddle seat equestrian, with both training and competition experience, but I had never practiced the discipline of dressage. I honestly thought it would be easy to learn dressage movements. Boy, was I wrong! Imagine being an expert in ballroom dancing, and starting ballet lessons when you're 64.

The following March, I traveled to Wylie, Texas, to train with Kai Handt. Kai owns and operates the United States Equestrian Federation (USEF) Center of Excellence, North Texas Equestrian Center (NTEC). He is the former USEF Para-Dressage Chef d'Equipe, and the only recognized Para-Dressage Coach at the Master Level in the United States. Kai knew I was a beginning dressage rider the moment I got on a horse, and he knew my dream was to qualify for the United States Para-Dressage Team and represent the United States in future Paralympics and World Equestrian Games.

During my first lesson, Kai told me my goal was challenging, but not impossible. I respected his honesty

243

and decided to work hard and smart to reach my dreams and achieve my goals. At that time, I had no idea of the risk, danger, sacrifice, and perseverance this transformational lifestyle commitment would require.

Can you appreciate how difficult it is for me, with no peripheral vision and no depth perception, to try to ride a precise 20-meter circle in the dressage arena? Can you imagine the fear I face in a schooling arena when I try to navigate around other riding teams, all traveling in different directions and different speeds?

To train seven days a week at NTEC, I closed my Bravo Performances piano studio in Jefferson City after 29 years of teaching. I am currently renting a room two-and-a-half miles away.

After a week of training, Kai partnered me with Cornet Noir, a handsome Bavarian Warmblood and former Fédération Equestre Internationale (FEI) showjumper. Two weeks later, Cornet Noir and I went to our first dressage competition for able-bodied equestrians and received very respectable and consistent scores above 67%, with a high score of 72.18%. We qualified for regional championships and earned several first and second placings. Kai told me, "It took three weeks for you to compete. For most people, it would have taken three or four years." After our exhilarating experience, I decided Cornet Noir and I were to be a team, and I bought him from Kai.

There is something about the outside of a horse that is good for the inside of a man.
—Winston Churchill

244

Three months later, I traveled to Gloucester, England, and became the *first* United States para-dressage equestrian with visual impairment to receive the confirmed international classification for competition from the International Blind Sports Federation.

During the 2019 show season, Cornet Noir and I qualified to compete in the *able-bodied* Region 9 Championship Classic, in Katy, Texas, and we won a championship title. All things are possible when one rides by faith, not by sight!

To pay for my expensive dressage training, I depleted my savings, sold my house, and sold or gave all of my possessions except for my 1917 Steinway grand piano and a few personal items. Because of Covid-19, in March, I stopped using Lyft or Uber services for the five-mile roundtrip to the training facility, walking 35 miles each week. Yes, walking in the darkness, freezing sleet, fierce wind, rain, slippery mud, and intense heat is grueling. Navigating around road construction obstacles and through rough off-road terrain is dangerous. As the song goes, "Whatever doesn't kill you makes you stronger."

Why will I never quit my para-dressage journey? My passion for horses fills my heart with unspeakable joy. Each horse I ride teaches me to understand myself and helps me discover the courage, strength, and mental toughness skills to conquer the adversities I will encounter in life. Horses, along with music, are the empowering freedom in my life.

Equestrian training has taught me these life lessons: Before I can master the horse, I must master my thoughts and emotions. I can only ride as well as I can guide. If *I* don't know where I am going, how can I expect the horse to get there? If I don't communicate to the horse where we are going, how can I expect the horse to know where to go?

Our journey, however, is not just about Cornet Noir and me. It's about how God will use us to bring glory and honor to His holy name.

God has blessed me with many incredible experiences and extraordinary friends who have encouraged me to pull myself up and off my pity pot and make my dreams happen. If you maintain a positive attitude, resolve to confront every negative situation, and follow the steps and strategies in my *Overcoming Adversity Training Plan*, you will become an expert at conquering adversity and triumph over your day-to-day struggles. If I can be an empowered, unstoppable force with which to be reckoned, so can you!

Regardless of your perspective about horses, leadership is everyone's responsibility, and applying the strategies leading to success in the discipline of dressage will not only help you become a leader in your own life but will also empower you to guide others toward happiness and success.

The three steps in my system are:

- Adjust your perspective.
- Take action.
- Stay on course.

One key strategy *to Adjust your perspective*: Do not let the past dictate your future.

246

As my coach, Kai, says, "Move forward, stay organized, control every step, go-go-go-get there, ride to win."

How does "not letting the past dictate your future" apply to *your* life?

One of your primary challenges in life is to become an expert in conquering adversity. Coping skills will help you deal with the stress of daily living. One of the most effective coping techniques is the problem-focused approach:

- Identify the problem.
- Analyze why victory has been unattainable so far.
- Choose a solution.

However, your coping skills alone won't protect you or guarantee that you stay committed to your dreams when you take action and move forward into the unexpected, the unknown, and the unseen.

What *will* help you get started and stay on course?

Believe in yourself, maintain a positive attitude, control your emotions, be 100% sure you are climbing the correct mountain, hold onto the unstoppable belief that you are capable of reaching your dreams, be willing to do whatever it takes to conquer every adversity, and then, no matter what happens, don't give up until you do. Keep moving forward instead of backward and you will conquer adversity.

If you don't take action to overcome adversity, you will find yourself defeated, not by the severity of the problem, but by your own negative attitude. People often ask me, "How are you able to continue to move forward despite embarrassing failures and overwhelming odds?"

I tell them, *every* day, I:

- Dare to dream a Mt. Paralympics dream.
- Believe the impossible is possible.
- Work hard, work smart to win.
- Ride by faith, not by sight.
- Never quit.

Life is a series of unpredictable events, and you have the choice to see them as overwhelming obstacles or empowerment energizers. If you want to experience a victorious Life's Ride, you must develop mental toughness skills for maintaining consistent control in inconsistent situations. **—Deborah McAlexander**

It's never too late to get up, get back on, and guide a triumphant ride on the horse life has given you. Every difficulty you successfully confront will strengthen your will, confidence, and ability to overcome future obstacles. Choosing the mindset to conquer and not be conquered will change you from a victim to a victorious Life's Ride Champion.

If Cornet Noir and I can conquer the adversity blinding our *Vision Beyond Eyesight*, so can you!

(In October 2020, Deborah and Cornet Noir participated in two Open Classes sponsored by the United States Para-Equestrian Association Emerging Athlete's Program scheduled at the Tryon International Equestrian Center, Mill Spring, North Carolina.)

Author's Notes

When I was 24 years old, I learned I would lose nearly all my vision, and my goal of becoming a concert violinist was no longer possible. Facing my first adversity, I set a new goal and studied piano instead, earning a Master of Music degree in piano performance from the University of Missouri-Columbia.

For 29 years, I owned an independent piano studio, Bravo Performances, for students of all ages and skill levels, and I became a nationally recognized music educator and pianist at corporate and social events. I'm a member of the Music Teachers National Association and Past President of the Mid-Missouri Area Music Teachers Association.

As a passionate horsewoman, I founded Vision Beyond Eyesight, Inc, a 501 (3) (c) nonprofit that provides support for the blind and visually impaired for their participation in equestrian activities. I give customized presentations on overcoming adversity to a variety of audiences on behalf of my nonprofit.

My beloved husband, Jack, died in 2017. Two years later, when I was 64 years old, I was introduced to the equestrian discipline of dressage. Before then, I'd only competed in saddle seat competitions, which are very different from dressage. Committing to a new goal, I closed my music studio and moved to Wylie, Texas, where Cornet Noir, my four-legged equine partner, and I are training to qualify for the United States Para-Dressage Team. We hope to represent the United States in future Paralympics and World Equestrian Games.

Cornet Noir's Bio

Cornet Noir, a handsome, dark bay Bavarian Warmblood gelding, was born in 2009 near Munich, Germany. He's by Westphalian Corlensky G, out of Bavarian Warmblood Sternstunde. He's a descendant of the famous Selle Français Cor de la Bryère, revered by most as the stallion of the century.

Cornet Noir spent his formative years as a show jumper, competing successfully on an international level across Europe, before moving to Texas and becoming my para-dressage partner.

Contact information:

Email: Deborah@visionbeyondeyesight.org
Website: www.deborahmcalexander.org
Facebook: Deborah McAlexander@Vision Beyond
                      Eyesight

Chapter 21

Grow Continuously

Les Brown

There's a saying that goes, *If the shoe fits, wear it*. But my mother, Mamie Brown, lived by a different saying: *If the shoe don't fit, make it fit!*

I remember Mama bringing home hand-me-down clothes at Christmastime from the families she worked for. One Christmas, she brought home some nice size eight leather shoes from one of the families. When I tried on the shoes, I couldn't get my feet into them because they weren't big enough.

When I told Mama I couldn't fit into them, I figured that would be the end of it. However, Mama called my sister, Margaret Ann, and told her to run some warm water into the bathtub and bring her some Vaseline. My sister did as she was told. As the water was running, Mama began rubbing my feet with Vaseline, then she stuffed my feet into those too-small shoes!

She instructed me to get into the tub and walk around in the water. "And you better not splash any water on the floor while you walking, either!"

I didn't know what the point was, so after walking around in the tub for a little while, I called Mama to let her know that the shoes still didn't fit. But she answered back, "Walk until they do!" I walked backward and forward for what seemed like forever. And, much to my surprise, after so many laps in the tub, the water-soaked leather became a comfortable eight-and-a-half—just my size!

> It doesn't really matter what happens to you. What matters is how you deal with it!

If it had been up to me, I would have just given up on having those nice leather shoes, because they didn't fit me. I didn't know they could be *stretched* into a perfect fit.

This reminds me of how people treat their dreams and goals. Many people refuse to stretch themselves because they feel *they don't fit* the requirements or can't measure up to the demands of what it will take to get there. The truth of the matter is, if you don't try, you will never know what you can or cannot do.

No matter what you think you know, you don't know enough about yourself to even doubt your own abilities.

According to the laws of aerodynamics, a bumblebee isn't supposed to be able to fly because its puny little wings are not big enough to hold up its large body. It's a good thing for bumblebees that they never studied aerodynamics and don't know about their ill-designed bodies. Despite what science says, they continue to fly anyway!

Sometimes you need to be *intelligently ignorant.* When you're targeted to be the victim of policies, politics, religions, cultures, ad environments that are stacked against you—systems put into place and intentionally designed to destroy your sense of self—you must be like the bumblebee.

Just like my shoes, you must **grow continuously!** There will be times in our life when you feel that you can't overcome the odds. However, when you continue to work on yourself and develop mental resolve, increase your skills, and surround yourself with nourishing relationships, you will be able to defeat whatever obstacles life throws your way.

253

Walk those laps around the tub of life until the shoe fits! Don't allow your circumstances to define who you are; create the circumstances you want for yourself! Stretch yourself until you fit the occasion and meet the requirements.

Standing in a wheelchair

I've listened to hundreds of thousands of motivational messages to expand my mind, to raise my own bar, to challenge myself to reach beyond my comfort zone. Why? Because I know *to have something you've never had before, you have to become someone you've never been before.*

There is no way to know when all of the motivation that I've filled myself up with will be put to the test of application. But trust me, those tests *always* come!

One day, my son, Patrick, was pushing me through the airport in a wheelchair. It was the first time that I'd been in public without being able to walk. As you can probably imagine, I was embarrassed. I hung my head down, hoping that people would not recognize me, but many did and greeted me warmly. I tried to hide my feelings, but their facial expressions were clear; they felt sorry for me and some wanted to ask what happened.

In the middle of my embarrassment, I paused to ask myself, *Why are you ashamed that the people you're going to speak to will know your condition?*

I realized that I needed to grow and stretch myself for this new challenge and I certainly rose to the occasion. Even though I spoke on stage from a wheelchair, I received a standing ovation from the audience. It really encouraged me to know that people did not judge me because of my condition. They were focused on my message, and although I could not physically stand up, I stood up through all of them when I received their ovation! My *hunger* stood up in me and in them.

You must realize things are going to happen to you in life—things you can't even begin to imagine. It doesn't matter what happens to you. What matters is how you deal with it! I no longer need a wheelchair to get around, but even if I did, I would not hang my head down. I will always hold my head up high!

I should never have cared about the stares of the people looking with their questioning expressions because I realize in that experience there was an opportunity for me to *grow continuously*. That is true for every experience, no matter how uncomfortable or humiliating.

Do not ever again let people—whether they're for you or against you—determine your level of growth and greatness! It's up to you to **grow continuously** *in every situation.*

Either you expand or you're expendable

To build my speaking business, I made so many calls that at one time I had a callous on my ear (people thought it was a big mole). I made over 100 calls each day. I even made calls on the weekends, when businesses were closed, just in case somebody was working overtime. Lo and behold, one day someone answered the phone on Sunday afternoon, and I met my first corporate client.

I had a dream of doing corporate training. As I methodically went through my list of contacts, I dialed the number for Michigan Bell corporate offices, a huge phone company. Someone picked up and I greeted him, saying, "Hello! My name is Les Brown. Do you, or someone you know, need a speaker to come in and motivate the salespeople to increase their performance?"

Bewildered, the person on the other end of the line said, "Do you know this is Sunday afternoon?"

I responded with just as much confidence as he'd projected bewilderment. "Yes, I do!" And I thought to myself, *Whoever's in working on the weekend is the person I need to talk to!*

255

He told me to come in the next morning so we could speak face-to-face. And that's how I landed my first corporate contract! I trained employees from Michigan Bell, Illinois Bell, Sprint, and AT&T—all because I was willing to do the things that others won't do.

No matter what your passion is or your dream is, you will have to learn to master it. A recent book came out with the message, "Average is over!" The question is: One day, will you look back in regret or delight for how you handled your dreams?

Maybe it seems extreme, making 100 calls a day to the point of getting a calloused ear. And you know what? It *was* extreme. I missed out on time with friends and family. I missed out on rest. I missed out on recreation, but that's what it took for the reward that I enjoy today. I don't regret what I missed. I delight in what I've gained, and how I've impacted the lives of billions of people around the world.

Make no mistake about it. If you're not growing, you're shrinking! We live in an area that literally operates at lightning speed. If you aren't plugged in, you're left out. Now, more than ever, it's critical to constantly reach further and *grow continuously!*

Alvin Toffler, the author of *Future Shock,* made a profound statement: "The illiterate of the twenty-first century will not be those who cannot read and write, but those who cannot learn, unlearn and relearn." He was right. Change is constant, particularly in this era. Being flexible and willing to *grow continuously* are the new basic requirements for success.

Advances in technology allow businesses to move at the speed of light and the direction can change in a millisecond. As the great Robert Shuler said, "We're living in a time where you either expand or you are expendable." You must be nimble enough to ride the waves of change or you will crash and drown. Maybe if I were in that same position today, working to build my speaking business, I'd send out 100 texts a day or make 100 social media connections or set up 100 webinars!

You need to understand what it is going to take to win at what you're pursuing. You must continue to train and educate yourself to remain relevant. *You must grow continuously. You've got to be HUNGRY!*

Sharpening your ax

Abraham Lincoln said, "If I had six hours to chop a tree down, I'd spend four sharpening my ax." The strongest tool *you* have is your mind. We must constantly sharpen and develop our minds. I agree with American's foremost business philosopher and writer, Peter Drucker, who said, "This is an era of accelerated change, overwhelming complexity, and tremendous competition, facing us all."

A huge proportion of America's jobs will be permanently eliminated in the next few years due to the rise of artificial intelligence (AI), technology, cheap labor abroad, and apps. This doesn't even count job losses that have happened due to the pandemic. This is a time in which job security no longer exists. This is a time when you must have the mindset of an entrepreneur, control your own personal economy, create your own jobs, and make your own impact! *We're coming to the end of work!*

According to the Department of Labor, *before* the COVID-19 pandemic, more than 20,000 people were losing their jobs each month. During the pandemic, a million people were losing their jobs each *week*. Many others had pay cuts or hours cut. Too many of these jobs will never return.

The days of the 40/40/40 plan have come to an end. Working 40 hours a week for 40 years to receive 40 percent of your income is no longer a realistic plan, and not even an option after the employment market imploded in 2020. This is the time to ask yourself, *What is my strategy for being here? What's my next move?*

Sadly, so many people focus on making a living instead of living their making. Studies show Monday mornings have a thirty percent increase in heart attacks. People wake up to the grim reality of spending another forty-plus hours at a dreaded job they despise, and they often die on the toilet. So, you have a choice: To reduce your risk of a heart attack, you can either stop going to the toilet on Monday mornings, or you can start living the life you desire to live!

You must *grow continuously.* Grow in terms of your talents and skills and every area of your life. Put yourself in a position to get out of that dead-end job! As Mamie Brown always said, "Used-to-bees don't make no honey!" Never mind who or what you used to be. **Who and what are you now?** This is the time that you must challenge yourself! This is the time to develop at least three core competencies—three things that you are skilled enough to do to get paid for them. Become the person who can earn a living doing what you love!

Jim Rohn, who helped millions of people improve their lives, once said, "Work harder on yourself than on your job."

In the middle of the 2008 economic recession, Warren Buffet was asked what the most important investment was that people should make. This is a man who has made billions of dollars in the stock market and real estate. He answered, "The most important investment you can make is in yourself.

Mr. Buffett was correct—*you* are your greatest asset.

As an asset, you must find ways to appreciate it. Sometimes it's still hard for me to believe that I earn more in one hour than most Americans will earn in an entire year. I don't share this to impress you, but to impress upon you that:

> *We shouldn't work to get paid by the hour;*
> *we should work to get paid*
> *for the value we bring to the hour!*

I want you to understand the power of investing in yourself. Knowledge is the new currency. Investing in yourself will yield the most profitable ROI (return on investment). Most of us never use the power that we have because we live in a world where we're told more about our limitations than our potential. This is why we must take the time to invest in our minds. We must acquire the knowledge to expand our vision of ourselves.

259

We must "sharpen our ax," sharpen our thinking and sharpen our skills. We must *grow continuously*.

Don't ever let fear hold you hostage. Now, more than ever is the time to grow, learn, strengthen your mind and your skills, and choose your future.

Author's Notes

I grew up with two mothers, the one who gave my twin brother and me life, and the one who gave us love, Mamie Brown. We grew up in poverty in Liberty, City, Florida, and people told me to give up my dreams—they said I was the dumb twin. I knew, however, that my dreams were possible and I refused to give up. I had a hunger to take care of my mother, and I wanted to make a difference in the world.

I started in radio, filling in for a DJ when he became inebriated and couldn't do the show, and then getting a radio show of my own. I became a community activist, a state legislator for three terms in Ohio, and then moved into training and motivational speaking, something I wanted to do my entire life. For more than 50 years I've been teaching people how to overcome their obstacles, become one with their gifts, and share those gifts with the world.

Contact information

Website: lesbrown.com
Facebook: The Les Brown
Instagram: @The Les Brown

www.ingramcontent.com/pod-product-compliance
Lightning Source LLC
Chambersburg PA
CBHW060256100426
42742CB00011B/1775